Garden Pools
Waterfalls & Fountains

Garden Pools
Waterfalls & Fountains

Andrew Booth-Moores

WARD LOCK

ACKNOWLEDGEMENTS

The publishers are grateful to the following for granting permission to reproduce the colour photographs: Pat Brindley (pp. 35 (top), 51, 54, 83, 86 & 91); Bob Challinor (p. 2); and Harry Smith Horticultural Photographic Collection (pp. 11, 15, 22, 27, 30, 35 (lower), 43, 47, 63 & 75). The cover photograph was taken by Bob Challinor, courtesy of Arthur Billitt of Clack's Farm.

All the line drawings were drawn by Stewart Perry.

First published as *Concorde Gardening: Garden Pools, Waterfalls & Fountains* in Great Britain in 1987 by Ward Lock, Villiers House, 41/47 Strand, London WC2N 5JE

A Cassell Company

This edition 1991

House editor Denis Ingram

Text filmset in Bembo by Paul Hicks Limited Middleton, Manchester

Printed and bound in Portugal by Resopal

British Library Cataloguing in Publication Data
Booth–Moores, Andrew
    Garden pools, waterfalls and fountains
    1. Water gardens
    I. Title   II. Series
    635.9'674   SN423

    ISBN 0–7063–7043–0

Frontispiece: A specially eye-catching variety of the Japanese *Iris laevigata*, 'Colchesteri' bears magnificent flowers 10–15 cm (4–6 in) across.

CONTENTS

PREFACE

Water gardening is one of the most popular pursuits of the modern gardener. The introduction in recent years of prefabricated pools and easily installed pool liners has not only made it possible for the majority of gardeners to construct a satisfactory pool themselves, but it has brought water gardening within the financial reach of almost everyone.

The intention of this book is to smooth the path of the newcomer to water gardening, and yet provide a handy reference for the more experienced. Water gardening can be a minefield to the uninitiated. It is hoped that the reader following the guidance given here will avoid most of the pitfalls, leaving time to enjoy the wonders of the pool.

A.B.-M.

PUBLISHER'S NOTE

Measurements are generally cited in metric followed by the imperial equivalent in parentheses.

In a few instances, owing to pressure on space, the imperial equivalent has been omitted.

CHAPTER 1

INTRODUCTION

Water gardening is a relatively new activity for the home gardener. While water certainly found a place in the past in the landscapes of famous gardeners like Capability Brown, this was scarcely water gardening as we know it today. The old masters merely dammed streams and created lakes to break up the landscape or else reflect its beauty. Only during the last 100 years has the active cultivation of aquatic plants for decoration been practised, and then widely only during the last 25 years. The cause of this revolution has been the introduction of the pool-liner and the preformed pool which have taken much of the heartache and hard work out of pool construction. Also, more is understood nowadays about the balance of life within a pool, so the much quoted passage of the father of English gardening, William Robinson, in his classic *The English Flower Garden* (1895) scarcely applies now: 'Unclean and ugly pools deface our gardens; some have a mania for artificial water, the effect of water pleasing them so well that they bring it near their houses where they cannot have its good effects. But they have instead the filth that gathers in stagnant water and its evil smell on many a lawn.'

Water in the garden has a peculiar fascination which is shared by young and old alike, whether it be tumbling over rocks and splashing into a pool alive with the red and yellows of goldfish, or in some sheltered nook supporting the broad verdant pads and brightly coloured waxy blossoms of the waterlilies. However, it is the position in which such a feature is placed that will decide more than any other single factor whether this ideal can be translated into reality.

Apart from the aesthetic considerations, those governing the welfare of plants and livestock must be taken into account if a healthy balance is to be subsequently maintained. All aquatic plants enjoy full uninterrupted sunlight and, although some will tolerate shade, these are usually the more sombre and less sophisticated subjects which the average gardener in the confines of a small artificial pool cannot spare the room to grow anyway. Fish likewise require as much sunlight as possible if they are to retain their brilliant colours and make satisfactory growth, although they do appreciate a shady corner in which to glide during the heat of a summer's day. But it follows that if a pool is placed in full sun, strong plant growth will result, which will in turn ensure that there is always plenty of surface shade available for the fish.

With a natural pool it is impossible to select its position or shape and it is foolish to attempt to convert such a natural asset into an artificial formal pool. Nature's ingenuity in placing such a feature in a natural setting is such that it can be only marginally improved upon, and then only by skilful planting rather than major structural alterations.

Practical considerations aside, the visual aspect must be carefully accommodated, for, even with a small area of water, the position in which it is placed can make or mar the garden. Time taken in combining the all-important practical requirements and aesthetic considerations is time well spent, for an ill-conceived pool constructed in the wrong part of the garden is a liability. Unlike other garden features, once sited it is difficult to move.

SITING THE POOL

Visually a pool should be in the lowest part of the landscape, whether that landscape be of magnificent proportions or the back garden of a suburban semi-detached house. The effect in both cases is similar. Water is ill at ease when situated higher than the surrounding ground, almost as if it is impatient to tumble to a lower area. Only when restricted by the sharp lines of formality does it seem at rest. Then it can be confined to a raised pool without offending the eye.

Obviously in the average garden it may be impossible or undesirable to place the pool in the lower part. Perhaps it would be overhung by trees or shaded by nearby buildings. In such circumstances the pool should be placed in a more amenable situation and, by the careful dispersal of excavated soil made to appear that it is in fact lower than it really is. This may sound difficult to achieve, but if surplus soil is used to lift the area behind the pool, or a rock garden is constructed to the rear, then the illusion is remarkably simple to contrive.

Protection from the prevailing wind can often be provided by rock outcrops or carefully planted shrubs in the background. Protection from the wind is not only useful during the winter, but also during the early spring when young plant growth is emerging. Later in the season, when aquatic plants are approaching maturity, wind protection will be invaluable in preventing the taller marginal subjects from toppling into the pool.

Protective planting can also create problems. During autumn, leaves of nearby deciduous shrubs will accumulate in the water unless the surface of the pool is protected with netting. This precaution should in any event be taken, for decaying vegetation in water generates toxic gases which can be lethal for fish, particularly during winter when the pool becomes covered with ice and these gases have no means of escaping into the air. Some leaves are especially toxic: those of evergreens like holly and laurel, as well as horse chestnut and willows. The seeds of the beautiful spring-flowering laburnum are particularly toxic, for they contain a soluble alkaloid which will very quickly spell the demise of the fish.

Weeping trees are often associated with water, but from the foregoing one can appreciate that they are not generally suited to poolside planting. Apart from the obvious problems that they cause, certain species, like flowering cherries and plums, are the overwintering hosts of the troublesome waterlily aphid, a menace that is as devastating to succulent aquatic plants as the black bean aphid is to broad beans. Weeping willow roots undermine the foundations of concrete pools and their leaves pollute the water with a toxic chemical akin to aspirin. Trees of a pendulous habit are for streams and riversides where their fallen leaves can be whisked away by the rains of autumn and winter.

A final consideration when deciding upon the location of the pool is the proximity of an electrical supply, for, if a fountain or waterfall is contemplated, the supply should be fairly close at hand.

FORMALITY AND INFORMALITY

While the position which a pool occupies in the garden is vital from both a practical and visual point of view, the design which the pool-owner adopts should not be neglected. Structurally sound pools in ideal situations are often spoiled by a lack of imagination in tying them in with their surroundings. While many gardens combine formality and informality satisfactorily in adjacent areas, and often to a limited extent within the same part of the garden, a pool must strictly adhere to the overall aspects of its surroundings. Formal beds and borders must be accompanied by a formal pool, while a cottage garden atmosphere dictates an informal feature.

A formal pool often serves a different function from an informal one, for in an appropriate setting it is often used to mirror the garden around it. Thus its surface may only occasionally be punctuated by groups of waterlilies and its margins graced with a restrained selection of marginal plants carefully placed so as to balance the visual aspect of the pool and yet not spoil it reflective qualities. Formality has little bearing upon the materials that the pool is constructed from. Prefabricated fibreglass pools, pool-liners and traditional concrete can all yield a first-class formal water feature, for this aspect of the design merely affects the surface, the shape that the pool takes and, to a lesser extent, the manner in which it adjoins the surrounding garden. Thus paving and walling can be used to effect in such a situation, while these materials scarcely have a use around the edge of an informal pool.

A formal pool should be a square, rectangle, circle, oval, or a combination of such symmetrical shapes, each counter-balanced so that the overall visual effect is one of equilibrium. The same applies to waterfalls or fountain features and, as intimated earlier, in certain cases with the planting too. However, that is not to say that the appearance of the pool should take precedence over the well-being of its inhabitants, for, as will be seen later, the correct ratio of plant types is necessary to ensure the sparkling clear water which all pool-owners desire. So in some cases a compromise must be made, although this should not substantially alter the overall effect of formality.

Informality in the water garden is more difficult to achieve and maintain satisfactorily. With a formal pool the gardener knows exactly where he is and can ruthlessly cull any plants that step out of line. This is not so easy to practise in the informal pool, for part of its charm is its tangled informality. Order must be kept and, while the regimentation of plants is not to be recommended, aquatics in an informal situation must be regularly kept in check. The pool itself, while being irregular in shape, should not be cluttered with fussy niches and contortions that are difficult to construct and frustrating to maintain. The water area itself should also seem to merge with the surrounding garden. Many gardeners believe that an informal pool should be planted liberally, with waterlilies obscuring areas of the water surface, and reeds and rushes tumbling in from the garden. While the plantsman will enjoy growing as wide a diversity of plant material as possible, the appeal of some areas of open water should not be overlooked. In an informal setting some reflections or movement of water can be equally desirable. Observe what nature does and try to emulate it.

NATURAL WATER

Fortunate indeed is the gardener blessed with a natural pond. He has a great advantage, for seldom need anything be done to alter its physical features: it is merely a question of dressing it with suitable plants. Often the marginal areas of a natural pool are inadequate and these may need altering, but apart from this it is prudent to leave as nature intended.

A golden conifer and distant astilbes give height to this rather formal kidney-shaped pool edged with limestone rock.

CHAPTER 2

CONSTRUCTING THE POOL

One can readily appreciate that what applies to the siting and design of the pool also applies to the internal structure. Careful thought must be given to the requirements of the plants and livestock and suitable accommodation provided. Once again, time must be taken to consider all aspects of the project, for a pool once installed is a very permanent feature. Adequate provision must be made for the various kinds of aquatic plants, for some prefer the shallows around the pool while others require much deeper water. Reeds, rushes and other marginal subjects like marsh marigolds and irises prefer to occupy shallow shelves at the edge of the pool. These should be about 23 cm (9 in) deep and of similar width if they are to accommodate aquatic planting baskets properly. The depth may seem excessive for plants that enjoy the shallows, but it must be realized that the planting basket will raise the plants close to the surface of the water. Waterlilies and other deep-water aquatics grow in the deeper central portion of the pool. Usually this is at least 38 cm (15 in) deep, but benefits from being deeper, particularly if you are considering overwintering fancy goldfish out of doors. Before deciding upon which pool to purchase or construct, it is as well to browse through one or two specialist aquatics suppliers' catalogues. You will then be better able to judge what provisions need be made for the fish and plant life you would like in your completed pool.

Modern materials have taken much of the hard work out of water gardening. No longer are puddled clay or gault pools constructed, when one used to have to line the excavation with soot to prevent earthworms from poking through the carefully laid finish. On warm days the area between the lawn and water surface had constantly to be watched so that, immediately signs of shrinkage appeared, water could be sprayed on to the puddled surface. Fortunately, those days are over, but it would be deceitful to suggest that constructing a pool was anything other than hard work, for even with modern materials a considerable amount of energy has to be expended. What modern materials have done is create options over construction, and ease maintenance after installation.

POOL-LINERS

Pool-liners are a popular form of construction, and justifiably so, for they are available in a range of sizes and materials that are within the reach of all but the most impecunious. The pool constructed from a liner can be as large and irregular as the gardener fancies and yet can be adapted simply to accommodate a bog garden as well. Most popular pool-liners consist merely of a sheet of heavy-gauge polythene or rubber material which is placed in the excavation and moulded to its contours. The water holds it in place within the pool while it is secured at the top by rocks, paving slabs or turves. Selecting the most suitable kind of pool-liner can be rather confusing; prices vary widely for products that, to the uninitiated, appear to be very similar.

The popular end of the market and consequently the cheapest pool-liners are those made from 500-gauge polythene in a light blue colour and made in various standard sizes. These usually make quite a small pool and can frequently be purchased from department stores as well as from garden centres and water-gardening specialists. However, they cannot be unreservedly recommended to the gardener who requires something fairly permanent. While it is quite true that, with exceptional care, a polythene liner is capable of lasting for 10 years or more, it is more likely that it will perish within three, the area between the water surface and ground level being bleached by the sun, cracking and falling away. In most circumstances the polythene liner has little to recommend it except as a cheap temporary home for fish and plants while the main pool is being cleaned out.

The pool-liners which fall into the next category are what one might call in the medium-price range and represent good value for the average newcomer to water gardening. They are usually of a polyvinylchloride (PVC) material and available in pastel shades as well as imitation pebble. While most are manufactured in handy sizes to make popular-sized pools, it is quite possible for a little extra expense to have one made to personal specifications. Likewise, in the more expensive rubber class, liners are often prepacked, but specific orders can be prepared too. The rubber liners are of the same material as used by farmers for irrigation lagoons and by local authorities for sailing and boating lakes. They have a black matt finish and are exceptionally durable, although some of the PVC ones are fairly comparable with their reinforcing welded terylene web.

Choosing the liner is one thing, calculating the size is quite another, for it always appears that you require a vast sheet for even quite a modest pool. The reason for this is that you do not just calculate the length and breadth of the pool, but the various areas that are going to accommodate marginal shelves as well. Sufficient surplus should be left at the top to allow an anchorage with stones or paving slabs and, when an irregular-shaped pool is envisaged, then calculations should be based upon a rectangle which encloses the greatest width and greatest length of the excavation.

All liners are installed in a broadly similar manner, those made from polythene being spread out on the lawn in the sun for an hour or two before installation in order to become more supple and mould to the excavation more readily. The hole should be scoured for any sharp objects likely to puncture the liner, for it should be remembered that, once water is added, the pressure of the liner against the walls and floors of the pool, and consequently against any sharp stone or twig, is such that it can be ultimately forced through the liner. To prevent this happening, it is useful to spread a layer of sand over the floor of the pool and along the marginal shelves to act as a cushion. A similar effect can be obtained for the walls by taking wads of newspaper and wetting them thoroughly before packing them against the walls in papier mache style. Recently a special polyester matting has been produced for use on very difficult stony soils. This is spun-bonded polyester fabric which will not decay and is placed in the excavation as a protective layer before the liner is installed. The various stages involved in making a 'liner' pool are shown in Fig. 1 (a–l).

As polythene liners have little elasticity, they are installed without water being added, but plenty of movement should be allowed for, so that, when the water is gradually introduced, the wrinkles can be smoothed out and the liner moulded to the contours of the hole. Rubber and PVC liners can be stretched across the excavation and weighted down with rocks or paving slabs. As the water is added and the liner tightens, the anchoring weights around the pool are slowly released until the pool becomes full and the liner moulds to its exact shape. Once the pool is full and as many of the unsightly wrinkles as possible have been smoothed out, superfluous material from around the edges can be trimmed, but do not neglect to allow sufficient for anchoring with stones or paving slabs. The pool is then immediately ready for planting, for pool-liners do not contain anything that is toxic to fish or aquatic plant life.

The pool liner also gives the gardener an opportunity to do what most other forms of construction are not flexible enough to allow, and that is to construct a bog garden as an integral part of the feature. All that is needed is a pool-liner that is larger in one dimension than necessary for the pool envisaged. This allows the development, at one

This tiny rock-edged pool forms a tranquil corner in a suburban garden. The plants include silver cineraria, ferns and hosta.

Below This pleasant pool is set against a background of water-worn limestone rockwork.

Fig. 1 Construction of pool with a liner. (*a*) A hose or rope is laid on the ground, to the required shape and size of the proposed pool. Commence digging, always cutting the turf or soil on the *inside* of the hose/rope, as shown here.

Fig. 1 (*b*) Proceed with the excavation, leaving marginal shelves as required 23 cm (9 in) wide and 23 cm (9 in) below water level. The pool perimeter is also cut back sufficiently to allow for the pool edging.

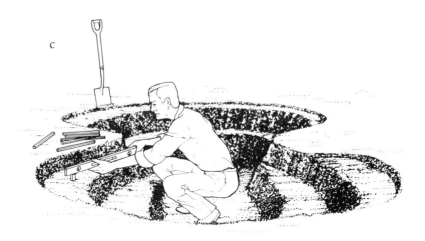

Fig. 1 (*c*) Short wooden pegs are inserted 90–120 cm (3–4 ft) apart around the pool and the tops levelled using a spirit level. It is important that the top edge of the pool be levelled as, on filling the pool, the water level will immediately show any non-levelness in the edging surface.

Fig. 1 (*d*) After the final shaping has been completed, the width and depth of the marginal shelves should be checked. The sides and floor of the excavation should also be checked for the presence of any sharp stones or roots which, if found, should be removed.

end, of a spreading, shallow-pool arrangement 30 cm (12 in) or so deep which can be readily converted into a bog garden. A retaining wall of loose bricks or stones separate the bog garden from the pool proper and retains the peaty mixture which is placed over a layer of gravel. This gives a moisture-retentive growing medium, but allows excessive wetness to drain from the roots of the plants. Water from the pool moistens the soil through the barrier, the soil level being a generous 2.5 cm (1 in) above pool level.

Fig. 1 (*e*) A cushion of sand 1.2 cm (½ in) deep should be placed on the floor of the excavation and on the horizontal surfaces of the marginal shelves. A layer of wet newspaper is used to cushion the sloping sides.

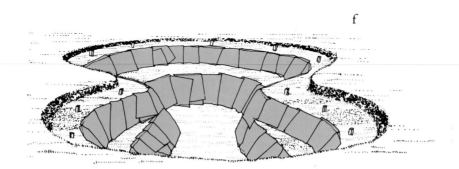

Fig. 1 (*f*) The finished excavation should be as neat and trim as possible – any irregularity in the surface will show after the liner has been fitted. The level pegs should be removed before the liner is laid.

g

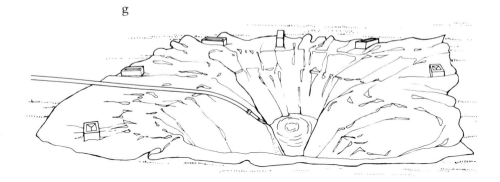

Fig. 1 (*g*) The pool liner is draped loosely into the excavation with as even an overlap as possible all round. Bricks or stones are placed on the overlap and water filling is then started by means of a hose.

h

Fig. 1 (*h*) As the pool fills, the stones should be eased off at intervals to allow the liner to fit snugly into the countours of the excavation. Some creasing is inevitable but it can be minimized by judicious stretching of the liner as the pool fills.

Fig. 1 (*i*) When the pool is full, the surplus liner is cut off leaving a 10–13 cm (4–5 in) flap. To ensure the liner does not slip, weight it down with stones.

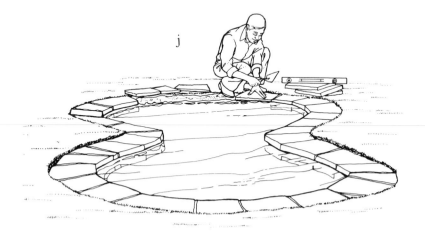

Fig. 1(*j*) The pool is then edged either with broken slabs or paving. The paving is laid on a bed of mortar 3 parts sand to 1 part cement.

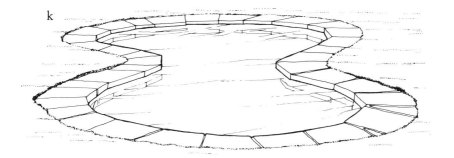

Fig. 1 (*k*) The finished pool. If cement has dropped into the water during construction work, the pool must be emptied and re-filled before planting and stocking with fish.

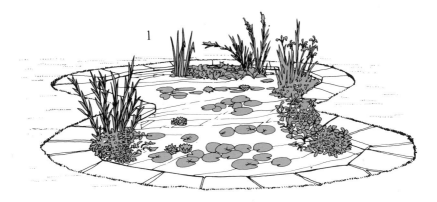

Fig. 1 (*l*) The pool is planted and, in time, will assume an established look. Fountains, lighting and other ornaments can now be added, if desired.

Thick and varied planting including dwarf conifers, variegated grasses, hosta and montbretia, give this water garden an established look.

PREFABRICATED POOLS

There are really two quite distinct categories of prefabricated pool: the fibreglass kind and those made of vacuum-formed plastic. The latter are the cheaper sort and are moulded in a tough weather-resistant plastic and have a roughish, undulating finish to simulate natural rock. While being inexpensive and readily transportable, they do have the disadvantage of flexibility which can cause problems during installation. Fibreglass pools are obviously entirely rigid and free-standing, and present no such difficulties during construction, but one must be very careful over the choice of design, for most are made by fibreglass manufacturers with little understanding of plant life and it is often the case that reeds, rushes and irises are expected to become established on a marginal shelf no more than 8 cm (3 in) wide, while the deeper areas of the pool will not have a sufficiently flat floor to place a single waterlily basket.

There are many different shapes and sizes to choose from and most can be obtained in a choice of colours, so it is wise to obtain a selection of catalogues from specialists and weigh up the advantages and disadvantages of each type before making what will undoubtedly be a sizeable investment. As in most walks of life, you generally get what you pay for and a higher-priced product will generally be of higher quality. Read the manufacturer's descriptions carefully, for some of the smaller pools are really rock pools which are intended to sit near the summit of a rock garden so that water tumbles down a cascade unit into a pool below. These are relatively inexpensive, but are not suited to most aquatic plants nor to accommodating ornamental fish. Fountain trays are also shallow and likewise can offer little to aquatic plant life, other than possibly a few submerged oxygenating plants. These are the small pools which accommodate a fountain in a confined space or serve as a receptacle to catch water spouting from a gargoyle. Even if they are deep enough to house a few aquatic plants, it would be unwise to do this, for when used for their proper purpose, water turbulence is such that none but the coarsest and most vigorous aquatics would survive.

Having decided upon a prefabricated pool, the next stage is to get it into the ground. If you ask the retailer how you go about it, he will probably tell you to dig a hole to the desired shape and then drop it in. In theory, this sounds quite simple, but in practice it is not so. What one has to do is to dig out a rectangle that will enclose the length and breadth of the pool and the greatest depth (Fig 2a). The excavation will, in fact, have to be substantially larger, for it must be remembered that room must be allowed around the edge for backfilling. The pool should be placed on a generous layer of sand and the shallow end supported on bricks. It must then be levelled from end to end and side to side by means of a board and spirit level (Fig 2b). The pool should be about 2.5 cm (1 in) below the surrounding ground, for during backfilling the addition of material packed tightly behind the pool will raise it slightly (Fig 2c). Start with the pool level with the ground and it will finish just proud, and then the edge will be difficult to disguise. The fact that the pool should be level from the outset and should be constantly checked during backfilling cannot be overemphasized, for a pool that is out of level leads to flooding in some places and unsightly exposure of the fibreglass in others. If the soil that has been excavated is in poor physical condition, discard it and backfill with sand or pea gravel. It is important that the medium used flows and fills all the air space, so that subsidence does not occur at a later date.

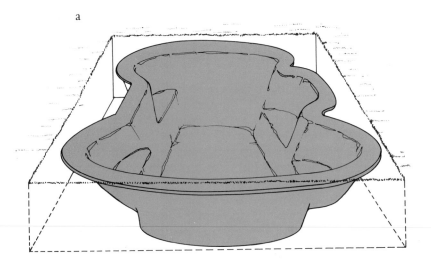

a

Fig. 2 Construction of a prefabricated pool. (a) Excavate a rectangular hole that will enclose the length and breadth of the pool and its greatest depth. To allow room for backfilling, make the length and breadth dimension about 23 cm (9 in) larger than the actual dimensions of the pool. The floor should be well compacted and a 2.5 cm (1 in) layer of sand spread and levelled.

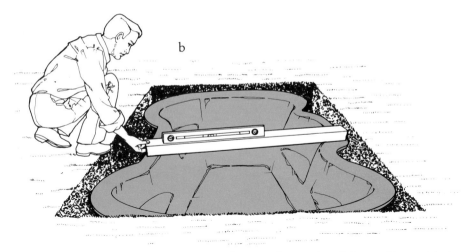

Fig. 2 (*b*) The pool must be levelled from end to end and from side to side by means of a board and spirit level. The top edge of the pool should be an inch or so *below* the ground level, because backfilling operations will tend to raise the pool slightly.

Fig. 2 (*c*) Commence to fill the pool and, simultaneously, to backfill with sand or sifted soil. The water level and backfill level should be kept the same to give maximum support to the pool. Particular care should be taken to backfill under the shelves.

d

Fig. 2 (*d*) The finished pool, edged with paving and established with marginal plants and waterlilies.

THE CONCRETE POOL

The concrete pool still has its adherents and rightly so, for a properly laid concrete pool is as good as any other and has the added advantage of being flexible in design. The design should embody all the aspects discussed, but is often difficult for the newcomer to visualize. So, before lifting the spade, take a length of rope or hosepipe and mark out the pool's shape on the ground. This ensures that the pool fits into the general scene and is of compatible size. The external shape can be marked out with the spade and the excavation begun. This marking-out to get an impression of the finished feature is not peculiar to concrete pools, for it will be realized that any pool made with a material that the gardener can mould to suit his whim can be assessed this way before excavations begin.

With a concrete pool it has to be appreciated at the outset that the excavation is going to be considerably larger than the finished pool, for room must be allowed for the layer of concrete. Indeed, the excavation should be at least 15 cm (6 in) larger than the finished pool to allow for a generous layer of concrete, and the soil should be rammed down

This small natural-looking pool is framed by a richly varied planting including variegated grasses and irises, hostas and primulas.

tightly to prevent any subsidence and ensure a firm base (Fig. 3*a*). A layer of heavy-gauge builder's polythene can then be used to line the excavation as a safety precaution against leaking, but also as a means of retaining moisture within the setting concrete so that it dries as slowly as possible. Newly laid concrete that dries quickly often develops hair cracks which are potential points of weakness.

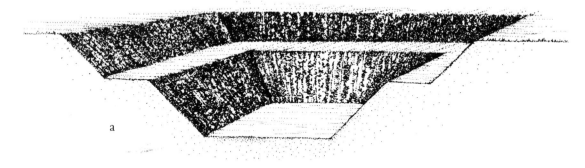

Fig. 3 Construction of a concrete pool. (*a*) The soil is excavated to the required shape. In this case it has been decided to have a marginal shelf running around the pool about 23 cm (9 in) below the surface – hence the stepped design. When excavating, remember to allow for the space taken by the concrete—at least 15 cm (6 in) all the way round.

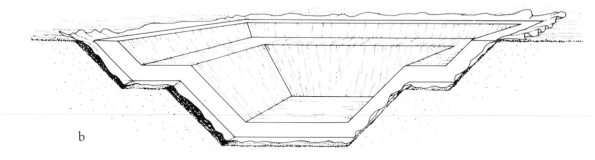

Fig. 3 (*b*) Having rammed the soil down firmly to ensure a firm base, a layer of heavy-gauge builder's polythene is used to line the excavation as a safety precaution against leaking and also to help retain moisture within the setting concrete so that it dries as slowly as possible. The concrete is laid to a depth of 10 cm (4 in) over the floor and up the sides. If the sides are very steep, it may be necessary to erect some formwork to hold the concrete while it is setting.

It is ideal if concreting can be carried out during one day as there is then less likelihood of a leak appearing. When this proves to be impossible, the edge of the previous day's work should be roughed up so that the new mix will key with it. Under no circumstances should the time that elapses between mixes extend beyond 24 hours, or leaks are almost inevitable. I prefer to get the concrete in already mixed. It

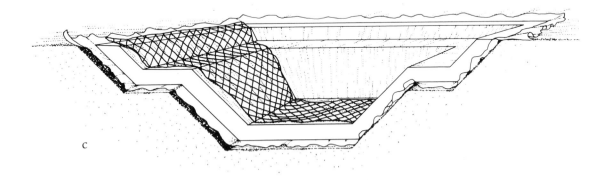

Fig. 3 *(c)* When the entire pool shape has been covered with its first layer of concrete, a reinforcing layer of 5 cm (2 in) mesh chicken wire is placed over the still wet concrete.

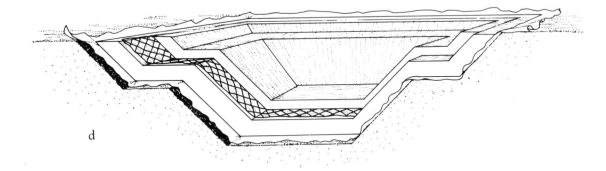

Fig. 3 *(d)* A final 5 cm (2 in) layer of concrete is then added and given a smooth finish with a plasterer's trowel. An hour or two after completion, cover all the exposed surfaces with wet hessian sacks to prevent the concrete drying out too quickly, a hazard which can easily occur in the hot summer months.

This tiny pool, with its small cascade, is almost hidden beneath its covering of waterlilies and surrounding fern, hosta and juniper foliage.

does present some problems, as once ordered the concrete will come irrespective of the weather. Notwithstanding that, ready-mixed concrete does have the great advantage of being consistently mixed, can have a waterproofing compound added to it before you get it, and saves the mixing time (which can mean the difference between the pool being completed in a single day and taking two or three). However, some people like to mix their own concrete; others do so on financial grounds, while a few feel that the lorry cannot get close enough to the site to make the upheaval that it inevitably causes worthwhile.

While mixing concrete is hard physical work, there is nothing terribly complicated or mystical about it. A good mixture consists of 1 part cement, 2 parts sand and 4 parts, 2 cm (¾ in) gravel measured out with a shovel or bucket. Mix a sufficient quantity to make the effort worthwhile, but do not be tempted to mix a vast quantity each time as it will be difficult to get the mix of even consistency. It is turned over and mixed in its dry state until a uniform greyish colour. If a waterproofing compound is to be added, it is done at this stage. Water is then added and mixing continued until the agglomeration is of a wet, yet stiff, consistency. A useful guide as to its readiness is to place a shovel into the mixture, withdrawing it in a series of jerks so that the ridges that are formed retain their character. If they collapse immediately, then they are either too wet or too dry and the mixture must be amended before use. Some pool-owners prefer their concrete pool to have a coloured finish and this can be provided during the mixing stage. Pigments, added at the dry-mix stage in quantities up to 10% by weight, give a good even colouring. Chromium oxide gives a green finish, red iron oxide a tawny red, cobalt blue a blue, and maganese black a black, while the use of Snowcrete cement and fine Derbyshire spar ensures a first-class white surface.

When the concrete is ready, it should be laid to a depth of 11 cm (4 in) over the floor of the pool and up the sides as well (Fig. 3b). If the pool sides are vertical or very steep, it may be necessary to erect some kind of formwork. Rough planks can be used in a formal pool with square or rectangular sides, but marine plywood and a series of props and strengtheners are necessary when an irregular shape has to be catered for. To reduce the risk of the concrete sticking to the formwork, it is advisable to grease or limewash it, although in practice a thorough soaking with clean water will have the desired effect. Once a layer covers the entire pool shape, a reinforcing layer of 5 cm (2 in) mesh chicken-wire netting is placed over the wet concrete (Fig. 3c). A final 5 cm (2 in) is then added and given a smooth finish with a plasterer's trowel (Fig. 3d).

An hour or two after completion, when any lingering surface water has disappeared, all the exposed areas of the concrete should be covered with wet hessian sacks to prevent the concrete drying out too quickly. In hot summer weather this frequently happens and, when drying is rapid, hair cracks appear. If the area to be covered is too large to contemplate covering with damp sacks, then the regular spraying of the surface of the concrete with clean water, from a watering can fitted with a fine rose attachment will have the desired effect. It depends upon the weather, but after a week or so the concrete will have dried sufficiently to be treated prior to the introduction of fish and plants.

Concrete contains a considerable amount of free lime which is harmful in varying degrees to both fish and plants. This dissipates with weathering, so, if your pool is constructed during late summer and is likely to remain empty throughout the winter, it will 'cure' itself. The same effect can be obtained by filling the pool with water and emptying it several times over a period of two or three weeks. At the same time it is recommended that sufficient potassium permanganate crystals be added to the water to turn it violet. What this latter achieves I am not quite sure, but I have yet to hear of a gardener who has experienced any problems with free lime after following this recommendation. However, the simplest method to overcome this potential problem is to fill the pool once with clear water and allow it to stand for about a week. Then empty it and allow it to dry. The surface can then be treated with a neutralizing agent like the universally known Silglaze. This is available as a white powder which is mixed with water and painted on to the concrete. Not only does it neutralize the free lime, but also seals the pool by internal glazing. Rubber-based and liquid plastic paints also prevent free lime from escaping when painted over the entire surface of the concrete. In most cases it is important to use a special primer first, or else the paint will flake and peel away, following a chemical reaction between it and the raw concrete. These paints are available in a number of natural and unnatural colours and while giving the pool a good waterproof finish, are generally considered to be rather expensive to contemplate for large expanses.

MINIATURE WATER GARDENS

Any receptacle capable of holding water is a potential water garden. Old galvanized water tanks, glazed porcelain sinks (Fig. 4a), or baths with their outlets plugged with putty are all extremely serviceable when sunk in the ground, although the first will corrode and leak unless protected initially with a good rubber-based paint. Discarded

a

Fig. 4 Miniature water gardens. (*a*) Sink garden. An old, glazed porcelain sink can be transformed into a water garden by coating it with an artifical stone mixture. First clean the sink. Then coat the outside with a bonding agent and, while this is still tacky, pat on a moistened mixture of 2 parts peat, 1 part sand and 1 part cement. Aim for 1.2 cm (½ in) thick layer all over the outside, over the lip and all the way down the inside surfaces. Leave to dry and harden for about 2 weeks. When planting be careful to select plants of modest growth.

vinegar and wine casks (Fig. 4*b*) also make excellent small pools when sawn in half, but wooden containers that have contained oil, tar or wood preservative should be avoided, as any residue that remains will pollute the water and form an unsightly scum on the surface.

No matter what container you use, it is advisable to give it a thorough scrubbing with clean water. Never use detergent for cleaning, as it is difficult to be certain when all traces have been removed. In tanks or sinks where algae have become established, the addition to the water of enough potassium permanganate to turn the water a violet colour will usually have the desired effect.

Planting can be undertaken in the same way as described for the conventional pool, but be careful to select only plants that are of modest growth. Fish can spend the summer in such a container but should be removed for the winter.

b

Fig. 4 (*b*) Tub garden. Discarded vinegar or wine casks also make excellent small-pool containers, when sawn in half and waterproofed inside with bitumen paint. A water tub will provide two or three goldfish with a pleasant home during the summer months but they should be removed for the winter.

Opposite, top This formal raised pool and fountain built in a striking modern style make a really strong garden feature.

Opposite, lower This long narrow raised pool provides a congenial home for waterlilies.

CHAPTER 3

FOUNTAINS AND WATERFALLS

Water holds a fascination for everyone, but never more so than when it is moving. With an appreciation of this, manufacturers have produced a whole range of equipment that can simulate a gentle tumbling stream, crashing waterfall or sparkling dancing fountain. Cascade or waterfall units made of fibreglass or vacuum-formed plastic are readily available in a multitude of shapes, sizes and colours. Some consist of a simple bowl with a lip, over which the water trickles, while others come in sections of varying lengths and shapes which can be joined together to form complex arrangements. Installation is simple, as the units merely need setting securely in position and the delivery hose from the pump inserted into the uppermost one before being fully operational.

A fountain can sometimes be incorporated with a waterfall by the use of a two-way junction on the pump outlet, but in most instances the pump is not sufficiently powerful to produce the desired effect. A fountain alone (Fig. 5*a*) is a much better proposition and, by the judicious use of jets with different numbers and arrangements of holes (Fig. 5*b*), some pleasing spray patterns can be obtained. Apart from straightforward fountains, ornaments depicting cherubs, mermaids and similar characters can be purchased, each designed to take a pump outlet so that water can spout from its mouth (Fig. 6), or a shell, or any similar object that they might be holding. Where space is very limited and there is insufficient room to accommodate a waterfall or fountain satisfactorily, 'masks' and gargoyles can be used with great effect. These are usually imitation lead or stone ornaments depicting the faces of gnomes, cherubs or sometimes the head of a lion, and are flat on one side to enable them to be fixed to a wall. Water is pumped up into the

Fig. 5 Fountains. (*a*) A sparkling fountain, achieved by means of a submersible pump, adds the interest of moving water to the pool environment. Care should be taken to site the fountain away from choice water plants such as waterlilies, which dislike turbulent water or fine spray on their foliage.

(*b*) Diagram showing how several different spray patterns can be made by means of interchangeable discs at the fountain head.

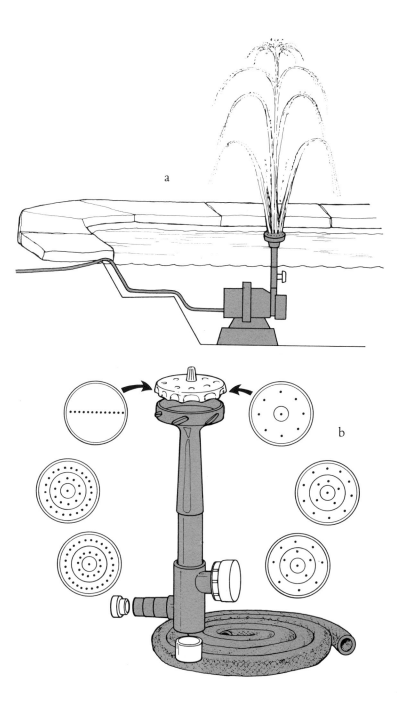

a

b

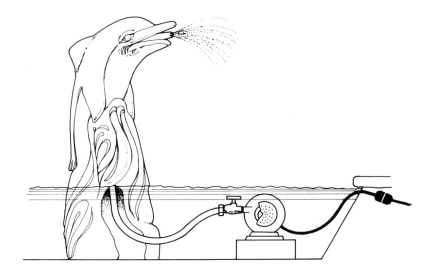

Fig. 6 Ornamental fountain. If a more decorative fountain is required, an ornamental fountain, such as this dolphin one, can be installed. Each ornamental fountain is designed to take a pump outlet so that water can spout from its mouth, shell or similar object.

'mask' and spews from the mouth into a pool below. While all these contrivances give us the pleasure of moving water, we must spare a thought for the plants beneath. Almost all aquatic plants with floating leaves dislike turbulent water or a continuous fine spray on their foliage, so any moving-water feature that is envisaged should be considered for one end of the pool and out of the direct line of choice plants like waterlilies.

CHOOSING A PUMP

While it is relatively simple to establish moving water in the garden, it can be somewhat hazardous deciding upon the necessary equipment without a little background knowledge or the advice of a fellow gardener with a similar feature. The catalogues produced by manufacturers and distributors of water pumps are so complex now that they can become difficult territory for the uninitiated, so advice should be sought from all quarters. Water gardening specialists usually reduce the chances of making an error by offering a selection suited to the ornamental pool, so their judgment should be trusted. When it comes to installation, sound advice can be obtained from the Electricity Council, for electricity is a good servant but a poor master and the inexperienced should not tamper with its installation, especially in the presence of water. You can, as a matter of course, help to protect yourself from electric shocks by using a circuit breaker. This is an attachment on the pump cable which is pushed into the plug socket of the domestic supply like an ordinary plug. If the pump or cable develop a fault, the electrical supply is immediately cut off. Even when the installation has been undertaken by an expert, the inclusion of a circuit breaker is a wise precaution.

Submersible pumps are designed to operate completely submerged in the pool and are silent and safe to operate. As they are merely placed into the water, there is no need for a complex plumbing arrangement or a separate chamber as with surface pumps. Generally, such a pump will consist of a cast body containing a motor although some recent models are made of non-corrosive materials like noryl. An input unit attached to this will draw water into the pump, often through a filter or strainer which will catch any debris and filamentous algae likely to block the pump. The cover of this unit will be removable and the collected debris should be periodically removed. Above the input is the adjuster assembly. This can comprise a single or double outflow to allow water to be discharged as both fountain and waterfall, although, as intimated earlier, one or the other is more desirable. Control can be exercised over both by the flow adjuster screw. In the case of a fountain, a jet with a series of holes in it will be attached to the outflow to create a spray pattern. Different interchangeable jets are available and these will give varying complexities and heights of spray. When a waterfall is envisaged, a length of tube sufficient to reach from the outflow to the head of the cascade is attached.

Some submersible pumps have a very small discharge and so it is important to judge the water flow required before shopping around. Most will provide an adequate fountain, but a surprising amount of water is required to operate a satisfactory waterfall. Most manufactured cascade units require an output of at least 1140 litres (250 gallons) per hour to put a thin sheet of water across their width, while 1365 litres (300 gallons) per hour is required to make a continuous filmy flow 15 cm (6 in) wide. If in doubt about the necessary flow, an indication can be gained by using water from the tap through a hose. The output from the hose can be assessed by pouring into a container for one minute. If the amount of water collected is measured in pints and that figure multiplied by 7.5, the gallonage per hour will be calculated. It is then a relatively simple matter to assess the flow required down the watercourse.

Installation of a submersible pump is quite simple, for, as described earlier, it is merely placed in the water. It is prudent, however, to set it on a level plinth, and in the case of a fountain assembly it is vital that the jet unit be just above the maximum water level. Connection to the electricity supply should be via a weatherproof cable connector to the extension lead. The most satisfactory arrangement is to have the cable connector concealed beneath a small paving slab. This means that the pump can be easily removed from the pool without disturbing the extension cable, if maintenance proves necessary. During the winter the pump should be removed in any event and this arrangement means that a pool heater can be conveniently installed in its place if desired. If a pump is not already in use, clearly an extension cable, with a weatherproof connector, will be required to reach back to the nearest electric point.

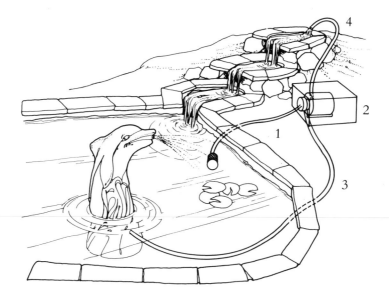

Fig. 7 Surface pump. A surface pump must be housed in a purpose-built, well-ventilated, dry chamber. Water is sucked up the suction tube (1) into the pump (2). Delivery from the pump in this instance is divided into two tubes; one goes to the fountain in the pool (3), and the other goes to the head of the waterfall (4).

SURFACE PUMPS

Surface pumps are preferable for some water gardens, especially where a relatively high 'head' of water is necessary, this 'head' being the vertical distance between water level and the highest point of discharge. If more than one fountain is desired, a surface pump is sensible and, of course when larger volumes of water than submersible pumps can easily handle are to be moved, then they become a necessity.

The range of surface pumps available is wide, but all need to be housed in a purpose-built, well ventilated, dry chamber (Fig. 7). This can be either above or below the pool water level, but, when above, a foot valve and strainer must be used on the suction tube to retain the prime. When the pump is accommodated below the water level, a strainer only need be used, as the prime is maintained by gravity. However, the pump must never be housed where the vertical distance from the water level exceeds the suction lift of the pump.

A surface pump consists of a cast body incorporating the motor, a suction tube with a strainer attached, and one or more delivery tubes according to the number of outlets being serviced. These tubes should be of adequate bore, without sharp bends, and as short as practicable. While the pump only has one outlet, separate delivery tubes can be attached by means of tee-pieces, but control valves are necessary to adjust the flow to each individual outlet.

FOUNTAINS

The simplest fountain is obtained by a jet unit attached to the outlet of a submersible pump, or to a figure or artifically contrived feature served by a surface pump. These are perfectly adequate for most gardeners, but the more technically appreciative and extrovert amongst us may wish to try some of the more adventurous systems currently available, especially those that incorporate varying spray patterns or coloured lighting.

The most exciting development in recent years has been the iluminated fountain. This is self-contained and provides a spectacular water display at night, yet during the daytime can be used as an ordinary fountain. Indeed, the addition to the conventional fountain is primarily a spotlight encased in a sealed alloy underwater lampholder unit. This is generally available with a choice of coloured lenses which give a single colour fountain. Alternatively, manufacturers have recently produced a colour changer. This is a revolving disc of different colour segments which automatically change the colour of the

Nymphaea pygmaea 'Helvola' is a gem for a small pool with only 15–23 cm (6–9 in) of water. It rarely grows more than 30 cm (1 ft) across.

fountain. The rotation of the colour changer can be adjusted to give slow or rapid colour change. While a conventional fountain with a standard spray pattern can be used to create a pleasing display, it has been found that, to give maximum colour density to the spray pattern, a thin columnar effect is best, and this is provided by a special jet with a larger number of fine holes. This jet can be controlled in the same way by use of the flow adjuster which is located just beneath the colour changing unit. The pump itself is attached to the lampholder unit, which in turn is securely fastened to a specially manufactured PVC base. Another type incorporates single colour lights immediately beneath the fountain jet, the water passing directly over and around the lamp before entering the jet.

Automatically changing spray patterns can be achieved by means of a device which can be attached to the pump. As many as 18 patterns are currently obtainable in a set sequence, with each spray pattern lasting up to 16 seconds and each complete sequence something like 3½ minutes. It is a fitting that is suited to both submersible and surface pumps, but the more powerful the pump the higher and wider the sprays produced, with a proportionate acceleration of the time lapse between each change of spray pattern.

Fanciful spray patterns can be created with special adaptors that not only vary the height and shape of the traditional fountain, but also produce unusual water patterns. Such an innovation is the bell fountain which, by means of a single adaptor, creates a unique globular spray pattern, almost like a glass bell in appearance. Single bells are fascinating, but triple bells from a single unit are quite remarkable. Not only are they breathtakingly beautiful during the day, but they can be easily lit at night. A similar feature can be created by the use of a fountain ring. This is a tubular ring with five or more adjustable jets which can provide varying spray patterns. The ring is attached to the outflow of a submersible pump. If you wish to recreate the geyser effect so spectacularly displayed in Geneva, but of course on a much smaller scale, then you can buy special foaming geyser jets. These only function successfully with larger pumps, producing a white water effect by combining air and water in the jet.

Adventurous fountain arrangements do not need to come readily packaged, for the ambitious gardener can create his own. One of the most imaginative that I have seen uses a series of bowls and a conventional fountain spray. Water is pumped up a tall central stem and then tumbles into a small bowl. Beneath this are bowls of the same shape and construction, but increasingly greater diameters. When the first bowl has filled, the water falls into the second and so on until it reaches the pool below. To ensure that the gently twisting curtain of water falls evenly from around each rim, it is absolutely essential that each bowl is level.

The problem created by such a feature, however, is one of excessive turbulence in the pool below. To counteract this, one must consider growing few plants other than the all important submerged oxygenating plants, or else arresting the turbulence by placing beneath the fountain a large ring which is of greater diameter than the lower bowl. Plants can then be grown in the relative peace of the perimeter.

Most fountains shoot water into the air, but a quite modest feature known as a pebble fountain is most restrained and yet very attractive. Although not technically a fountain, it utilizes the same components as the conventional fountain. In appearance it is a contained area of sizeable attractive pebbles or cobbles through which water constantly bubbles. It is easy to maintain and does not need either aquatic plant life, fish or snails. Essentially it consists of a small concrete chamber which is waterproof and can accommodate sufficient water to enable a simple submersible pump to operate. A framework of iron bars is placed across the top and this supports fine mesh netting. On top of this a generous layer of washed pebbles or cobbles is placed and the pump outlet drawn up until it is at the surface of the stones. Water bubbles up through the pebbles, creating a cool refreshing effect. As evaporation is rapid, the chamber beneath will require regularly topping up with fresh water.

WATERFALLS

The construction of a simple waterfall is shown in Fig. 8.

Mention has already been made of waterfall cascade units. Like prefabricated pools these are moulded in plastic or fibreglass and are available in both natural and unnatural colours. They are simple to install, for all that is required is that they be level from side to side, and with the lip protruding sufficiently to enable the full body of water to be emptied into the pool rather than on to the surrounding ground (Fig. 9). The hose from the outlet of the pump is then carefully hidden, but emerges at the summit of the unit and the water gently tumbles down.

A waterfall does not have to be prefabricated to be successful and in certain circumstances it is desirable that it is not so. Prefabricated units are not necessarily of the shape or length desired and, when something special is needed, the waterfall can be made with concrete, although some suppliers suggest that a presentable feature can be constructed

Fig. 8 Simple waterfall. Section diagram showing how a simple waterfall can be made by means of a submersible pump, to which is attached a length of flexible tubing. Note that the pump is set on a level plinth.

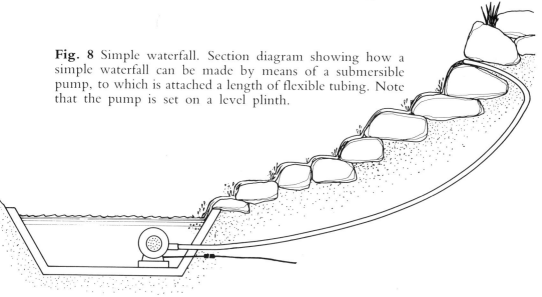

Fig. 9 Preformed waterfall. Waterfall or cascade units can be made of plastic or fibreglass. They are simple to install; all that is required is that they be level from side to side, and with the lip of the lowest basin protruding sufficiently so that the water empties directly into the pool water and not on to the edging of the pool.

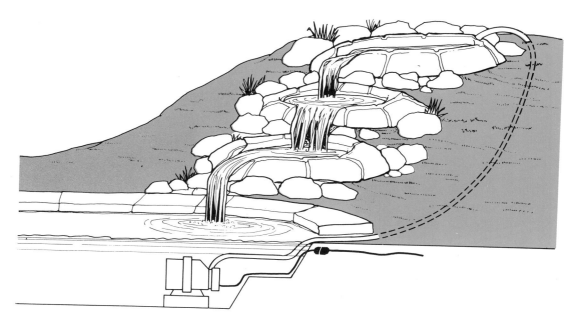

'Rose Arey' is typical of the many lovely larger hybrid waterlilies suitable for bigger pools with deeper water.

using a pool liner. While this may be possible, it can by no stretch of the imagination be deemed easy (Fig. 10).

A purpose-built waterfall will obviously have to conform visually to the site and fulfil its function of delivering water from a higher area to a pool below. The upper part, or header pool, should be reasonably deep, but will not be capable of supporting aquatic plant life or fish. Each small basin forming the cascade should be so constructed that, when the water is switched off, a small quantity remains in each. This can be done by tipping the leading edge up, so that water only flows over the lip when a reasonable quantity is being pumped. Concrete of the same consistency as is used for pool construction is used to form the waterfall, which like the pool benefits from being 15 cm (6 in) deep. While the concrete is still wet, a more natural effect can be created by the addition of rockwork set into the concrete to create the faces of each small basin. This rockwork can similarly be used around the edges to hide their harshness. It is important that these edges be level in the horizontal plane so that water is distributed evenly throughout each basin. Waterfalls of varying kinds can be constructed that vary considerably from the traditional form. One of the most interesting of these is the grotto, where a pool is constructed with a background of similar appearance to a rock garden. A small cavern is constructed at

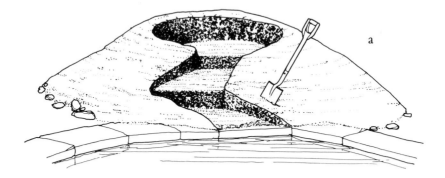

Fig. 10 Waterfall construction using a liner. A waterfall constructed with a pool liner offers greater flexibility in design than does a preformed unit. It is, however, much more difficult to construct and you would be well advised to seek professional help in making this feature.
(*a*) On soil that is well consolidated, cut out the steps of the watercourse as required.

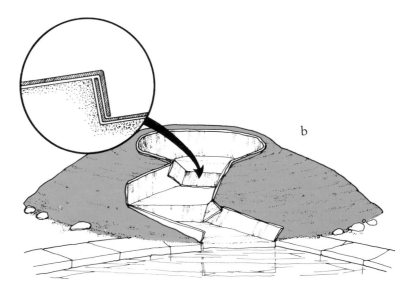

b

Fig. 10 (*b*) Lay the liner into the excavated watercourse. The sides of the liner must be kept above the anticipated maximum water level. Each small basin forming the cascade should be so constructed that, when the water is switched off, a small quantity remains in each.

(*c*) Stones, bedded on mortar, are then laid down to form the watercourse. The positioning of the stones will determine the type of fall. Further stones can then be added around the edges to create a natural-looking watercourse. Finally, the surrounding ground on either side of the waterfall can be made into a rockery, thus completing the feature.

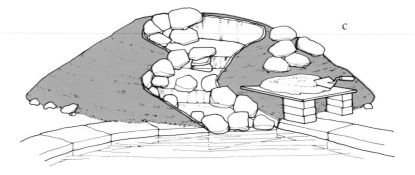

c

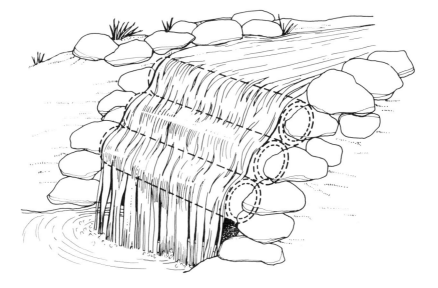

Fig. 11 Water staircase. A mini-version of the latter day water staircase beloved of French and Italian gardeners. Here the staircase is achieved by sizeable concrete drainage pipes set in a bed of concrete one behind the other, each pipe slightly above the next. To camouflage the ends, fill them with concrete or soil and then cover them with plants or rocks.

the summit and contains a pump outlet surrounded by well washed pebbles or cobbles. These stones extend down the watercourse, over which water flows with the aid of a simple submersible pump. The illusion is that the water is emerging from within the grotto. When tastefully dressed with ferns and other moisture-loving plants around its edges, it makes a very attractive if somewhat mystical feature.

From modesty to exuberance and one can scarcely get more exuberant than a water staircase (Fig. 11). Beloved of French and Italian gardeners years ago, this feature can be tastefully recreated in the small garden. The idea behind a water staircase is that it appears as a staircase of sparkling, silvery water. This can be achieved in the modern garden by the use of sizeable concrete drainage pipes set in a bed of concrete one behind the other, each pipe slightly above the next. Thus one has a staircase with rounded steps, but to disguise the edges it is necessary to fill the hollow ends of the pipes with concrete or soil and suitably hide them with plants. If the pipes are new they may require treating with a pool sealant.

The effect of a water staircase can be marvellous, but only when sufficient water is flowing over it. If such a feature is envisaged, do not skimp on the purchase of a pump of sufficient size. The whole concept depends upon the volume of water being sufficient.

FILTERS

Most pumps have filters attached to their input in order to gather debris and algae that are likely to cause mechanical problems. Some recent models even incorporate an integral filter which is intended to clarify the water rather than just catch debris. However, it is perfectly possible to fit special filter units to most ordinary classes of submersible pumps in order to extract water discolouring algae. These units should not, however, be used in an attempt to replace the natural balance between various kinds of aquatic plant, for this is the perfect answer for any pool. However, temporary problems do arise and then a filter can undoubtedly assist, particularly in the smaller pool where a natural balance is more difficult to establish.

The pool filter usually looks like a deep tray. In fact, it is two trays, one inside the other, the inner one containing a foam filter element which is covered with gravel or charcoal. The pump is connected through the outer tray and draws water in through the gravel or charcoal, and then through the filter elements into the pump for discharge as a fountain or waterfall. Debris and algae collect in the medium in the inner tray and can regularly be changed and disposed of. Another system uses a small filter, or algae trap, at the discharge side of the pump. The filter must be regularly changed.

Biological filters are a different proposition. These depend upon the water passing through a gravel or foam medium on which useful bacteria develop. These are capable of converting waste organic matter into plant nutrients. Biological filters operate outside the pool, usually at the summit of a waterfall where they can be suitably hidden – water from the pool being pumped through the filter and allowed to discharge into the waterfall. Alternatively it can be placed close by the pool and the water circulated and returned immediately. Biological filters have to be operated continuously for if the filter is allowed to dry out the bacteria perish. Such a filter is not used during the winter; it is just cleaned and put away until the following spring.

Caltha palustris, the marsh marigold here in its single and double-flowered forms, brings sunny colour to the bog garden.

· CHAPTER 4 ·

WATERLILIES AND DEEP WATER AQUATICS

Water gardening is unlike any other kind of gardening, for when planting a pool the gardener is creating a whole new underwater world in which plants, fish and snails depend upon one another to provide the basic requirements necessary for their continued existence. Submerged oxygenating plants replace the oxygen that has been lost in respiration. By using up all the available mineral salts, they compete with the slimes, algae and other primitive forms of plant life, which turn the water thick and green. Thus the slimes and algae are starved out of existence. Floating plants assist by shading the surface of the water and making life intolerable for any of the green water-discolouring algae which try to dwell beneath them. As one can well imagine, the surface shade so necessary for a healthy balance within the pool can to some extent be provided by waterlilies. However, this is not the main reason for gardeners wishing to grow these gorgeous subjects, for throughout the summer they provide a dazzling display of beautifully sculptured blossoms in almost every shape, size and colour imaginable. There are pygmy varieties that can be grown in a sink, right through to vigorous kinds that are only suited to a lake or large pool in a public park.

Like all aquatic plants, waterlilies can be planted successfully from spring until late summer, using properly designed baskets and good garden soil (Fig. 12). It is important when collecting soil to avoid getting any old leaves or weeds mixed in with it, as these will only decompose and foul the water. Soil from land that has been recently dressed with artificial fertilizer should be similarly avoided, as this too will pollute the water. Plant the waterlily with just the 'nose', or growing point, protruding above the soil and then cover the surface of the basket with a generous layer of pea gravel to prevent the fish from stirring up the mud. Before putting the waterlily in the pool, soak the basket throughly with water from a watering can fitted with a fine rose. This will drive most of the air out of the growing medium and prevent clouds of bubbles and associated debris from being released into the pool. It is also useful to remove all the adult leaves from waterlilies (or indeed any lily-like aquatics) before planting, as these give the plants buoyancy and can lift them out of the basket. When placing waterlilies

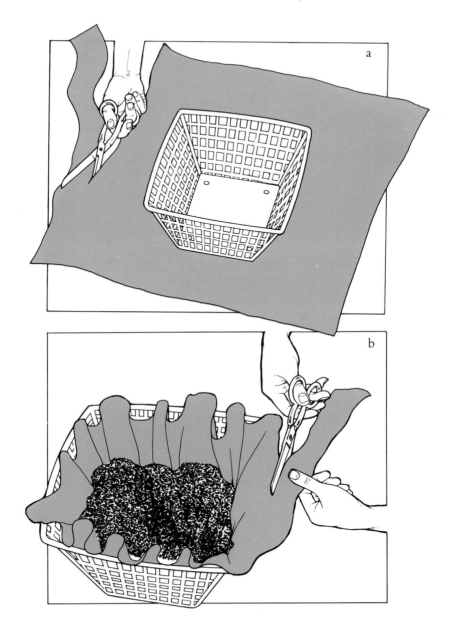

Fig. 12 Planting waterlilies. (*a*) Use properly designed baskets and good garden soil or a heavy loam compost. First cut out a square of hessian to line the planting basket.
(*b*) Half fill the basket with soil/compost and trim off the excess hessian.

(*c*) Plant the lily firmly in the soil/compost.
(*d*) Continue to fill the basket with soil/compost to within an inch or so of the top, and then cover with a layer of pea shingle.

in the pool, it is essential to situate them well away from a fountain or waterfall and in a really sunny position, for they are intolerant of shade or turbulent water.

The striped sword-shaped leaves of *Iris pseudacorus* 'Variegata' create a telling feature at the waterside.

WATERLILIES

All the following waterlilies (*Nymphaea*) are suited to the modern water garden. The measurements indicate the depths at which each cultivar can be successfully accommodated.

'Alaska'	A very hardy modern variety having white blossoms with bright yellow stamens. 60–90 cm (2–3 ft).
'Albatross'	Medium growing white-flowered waterlily with bright green leaves that are purplish when first produced. 30–60 cm (1–2 ft).
'Amabilis'	Also known as 'Pink Marvel', this waterlily has large star-shaped salmon-pink flowers that age to soft rose. 45–60 cm (1½–2 ft).
'American Star'	An exciting new introduction from the United States with beautiful star-shaped pink blossoms and a delicate fragrance. Unlike most standard varieties, this holds its flowers well above the foliage, very much like the tropical varieties. 30–60 cm (1–2 ft).
'Attraction'	Only recommended for the larger pool. A vigorous kind with large garnet-red flowers flecked with white. 60 cm–120 cm (2–4 ft).
'Aurora'	The most popular of the chameleon cultivars. This has creamy buds which open yellow and then pass through orange to blood red. 30–45 cm (1–1½ ft).
'Conqueror'	Bright crimson cup-shaped blossoms flecked with white. The foliage emerges purple but eventually turns green. 45–60 cm (1½–2 ft).
'Ellisiana'	A very free-flowering kind with wine-red flowers that sport vivid orange stamens. 30–60 cm (1–2 ft).
'Froebeli'	Deep blood-red flowers with orange stamens and dull purplish-green leaves. 45–60 cm (1½–2 ft).

'Gonnere'	This white flowered waterlily is sometimes listed as 'Crystal White'. Its fully double globular flowers float like snowballs amongst bright green foliage. 45–75 cm (1½–2½ ft).
'Graziella'	This is another chameleon variety with orange-red blossoms that darken with age. 30–60 cm (1–2 ft).
'Hermine'	Pure white tulip-shaped blossoms and distinctive dark green oval leaves. 45–75 cm (1½–2½ ft).
'James Brydon'	Large, fragrant crimson paeony-shaped blossoms with deep orange stamens. 45–90 cm (1½–3½ ft).
Laydekeri hybrids	This very useful group of hybrids all flourish in a depth of 30–60 cm (1–2 ft) of water.
laydekeri 'Alba'	White flowers with yellow stamens and a fragrance reminiscent of a freshly opened packet of tea.
laydekeri 'Fulgens'	Crimson blossoms with reddish stamens.
laydekeri 'Purpurata'	Rich red flowers with bright orange stamens are produced in abundance. One of the best red waterlilies for the small pool.
Marliacea hybrids	Invaluable waterlilies for the larger pool where the water depth is between 45 and 75 cm (1½–2½ ft).
marliacea 'Albida'	Pure white fragrant blossoms and handsome deep green leaves.
marliacea 'Chromatella'	Bright canary-yellow blossoms and olive-green foliage liberally splashed and stained with maroon and bronze.
marliacea 'Flammea'	Fiery red blossoms float amongst olive green leaves that are heavily mottled with chocolate and maroon.
'Masaniello'	Fragrant rose-pink cup-shaped blossoms which age to deep carmine. 45–90 cm (1½–3 ft).
'Mrs Richmond'	Pale rose-pink flowers which age to crimson. Bright yellow stamens. 45–75 cm (1½–2½ ft).

Odorata hybrids	A variable group of hybrids derived from the popular sweet scented waterlily, *Nymphaea odorata*. All are fragrant.
odorata 'Firecrest'	Deep pink flowers with red-tipped stamens and striking purplish leaves. 45–90 cm (1½–3 ft).
odorata 'Sulphurea'	Star-like canary-yellow flowers and dark green heavily mottled leaves. The form 'Grandiflora' is larger and finer in all respects. 45–60 cm (1½–2 ft).
odorata 'William B. Shaw'	Creamy-pink blossoms with a red internal zoning held above the water. 45–60 cm (1½–2 ft).
'Pink Sensation'	Fragrant and free-flowering with enormous star-shaped blossoms of bright pink. 45–75 cm (1½–2½ ft).
Pygmaea hybrids	These pygmy waterlilies are ideal for sinks, troughs and small pools with no more than 30 cm (1 ft) of water.
pygmaea 'Alba'	A really miniature white flowered waterlily, each blossom scarcely 2.5 cm (1 in) across. Tiny dark green lily pads with purplish undersides.
pygmaea 'Helvola'	A tiny canary-yellow waterlily with heavily mottled olive-green leaves.
pygmaea 'Rubra'	Little blood-red flowers and tiny purplish-green floating foliage.
'Rene Gerard'	Rose-pink blossoms darkening to crimson towards the centre. 45–75 cm (1½–2½ ft).
'Robinsoniana'	This old variety, which was introduced towards the end of the last century, more or less disappeared from cultivation. It is now available from nurseries under the more dubious name of 'Robinsonii'. Beautiful star-shaped blossoms of a coppery-red hue and olive-green foliage. 45–60 cm (1½–2 ft).
'Rose Arey'	Beautiful star-like rose-pink blossoms with a delicious aniseed fragrance. 45–75 cm (1½–2½ ft).

'Sioux'	Very similar to 'Aurora' having yellow flowers that pass through orange to red with age. Dark olive-green leaves with a purplish mottling. 30–45 cm (1–1½ ft).
'Virginalis'	Semi-double blossoms of pure white with yellow stamens. 45–75 cm (1½–2½ ft).

DEEP WATER AQUATICS

Although waterlilies are the most important group of deep water aquatics, they do not have an automatic right to the deeper areas of the pool. There are a number of other deep water aquatics well worth considering for this.

Aponogeton distachyus (Water hawthorn)	Small floating dark green more or less oblong leaves provide a perfect foil for the vanilla scented pure white blossoms with conspicuous black stamens. A most reliable aquatic which flowers from late spring until the first autumn frosts. 30–90 cm (1–3 ft).
Nuphar lutea (Brandy bottle, yellow pondlily)	Similar in habit to the true waterlily, but with smaller yellow flowers. Only worth growing as a substitute for waterlilies in shaded or running water. Summer. 30 cm–240 cm (1–8 ft)
Nymphoides peltata (Water fringe)	A lovely little aquatic with delicately fringed buttercup-like flowers and small waterlily-like leaves. Summer. Sometimes grown under the name *Villarsia nymphoides*. 30–75 cm (1–2½ ft).

CHAPTER 5

MARGINAL PLANTS

Marginal plants, as their name implies, grow in the shallow water at the pool's edge and can either be grown in planting baskets, like waterlilies, or in soil that has been placed directly on the marginal shelf. This latter proposition is not ideal as the more rampant plants will crowd out the less vigorous and often more desirable subjects. In the past it has sometimes been difficult to avoid planting directly on to the marginal shelf, especially in pre-formed pools. It seems that most designers of fibreglass pools are not water gardeners, for the shelves are often narrow and curved making it difficult to accommodate a traditional square planting basket. To overcome this problem one enterprising manufacturer now produces narrow contoured baskets which fit snugly on to the shelves of all popular designs. Marginal plants are of no value in maintaining a balance and are planted purely for decoration. While most gardeners wish to grow as many aquatic plants as they can fomfortably accommodate, the water is itself an atractive feature, and sufficient uncluttered area must be allowed for reflections. An over-planted pool detracts from its surroundings, while it should essentially be a feature that complements them. Spotty or regimented planting cannot be tolerated either. Marginal plants should be grouped together like plants in an herbaceous border, several of the same variety being accommodated in a single basket. Apart from being aesthetically undesirable to have mixed plantings, it is impractical, for the more vigorous plants to outgrow their weaker neighbours and create difficulties.

Measurements denote the average heights of mature plants.

MARGINAL PLANTS

Acorus calamus 'Variegatus' (Variegated sweet flag)	Handsome green, cream and rose striped foliage. Insignificant brownish flowers. 45–75 cm (1½–2½ ft).
A. gramineus 'Variegatus'	Diminutive grassy form of acorus with cream and green striped leaves. 23–30 cm (9–12 in).

Butomus umbellatus (Flowering rush)	Spreading umbels of rose pink flowers are produced amidst slender triquetrous foliage. Late summer. 45–90 cm (1½–3 ft).
Calla palustris (Bog arum)	Pure white flowers like tiny sails amidst a sea of dark green glossy foliage. Spikes of succulent red berries follow in the autumn. Spring. 23–30 cm (9 in–1 ft).
Caltha palustris Marsh marigold, (kingcup)	A spring flowering waterside plant with striking heads of large golden blooms. 30–75 cm (1–2½ ft).
C. palustris alba	Is a smaller flowering white form of marsh marigold. Spring. 23–30 cm (9 in–1 ft).
C. palustris 'Flore Pleno'	Is a fully double yellow cultivar. Spring. 23–30 cm (9 in–1 ft).
Glyceria aquatica 'Variegata' (Variegated water grass)	Handsome cream and green striped leaves with a rosy suffusion in spring. 75–90 cm (2½–3 ft).
Iris laevigata	The true blue aquatic iris. Summer. Many fine culivars have been raised. 60 cm (2 ft).
I.l. 'Albopurpurea'	Attractive blossoms with mauve and white petals which blend and merge into one another. Summer. 60 cm (2 ft).
I.l. 'Colchesteri'	Handsome blooms with contrasting petals of violet and white. Summer. 60 cm (2 ft).
I.l. 'Muragumo'	Deep blue lined with gold. Unlike the ordinary *I. laevigata* this has six petals instead of three. 60 cm (2 ft).
I.l. 'Snowdrift'	The best white aquatic iris available. Summer. 60 cm (2 ft).
I. pseudacorus (Yellow flag)	Strong growing yellow flag iris. Summer. 60 cm–1.5 m (2–5 ft).
I. versicolor	A splendid fellow with violet blue flowers veined with purple and with a conspicuous patch of yellow on the falls. Summer. 60 cm (2 ft).

I. v. 'Kermesina'	Georgeous deep plum blooms with distinctive yellow markings. Summer. 60 cm (2 ft).
Juncus effusus 'Spiralis'	A curiously malformed plant with stems like a Harry Lauder walking stick. 45 cm (1½ ft).
Menyanthes trifoliata (Bog bean)	Decorative white fringed flowers above dark green trifoliate leaves not unlike those of a broad bean. Late spring. 30 cm (1 ft).
Mimulus ringens	A delicate looking plant with much branched slender stems and dainty powder blue flowers. Summer. 45 cm (1½ ft).
Myosotis scorpioides (Water forget-me-not)	Just like the familiar bedding forget-me-not, but perennial and with softer hairless leaves. Bright blue. Late spring and early summer. 23–30 cm (9 in–1 ft).
Orontium aquaticum (Golden club)	Handsome glaucous foliage and erect narrow spikes of white and yellow blooms held just above the water. Sometimes listed as a deep water aquatic as it will also tolerate deep water. Late spring and early summer.
Peltandra virginica (Arrow arum)	An unusual plant with narrow sail-like spathes of a pea-green colour borne amidst dark green glossy arrow-shaped foliage. Late spring, early summer. 75 cm (2½ ft).
Pontederia cordata (Pickerel)	A plant of noble proportions producing numerous stems each consisting of a large shiny green leaf and a leafy bract from which a spike of soft blue flowers emerges. Late summer. 60–90 cm (2–3 ft).
Preslia cervina	A small spreading plant with slender erect stems densely clothed in small lanceolate aromatic leaves, and crowned during late summer with stiff whorled spikes of dainty lilac flowers. 30 cm (1 ft).

The pickerel, *Pontederia cordata*, produces erect spikes of blue flowers, which continue well into autumn.

Sagittaria japonica (Arrowhead)	Bold clumps of fresh green arrow-shaped foliage and symmetrical spires of snow-white flowers. Summer. 60 cm (2 ft).
Flore-Pleno'	*The striking double form 'Pleno' has flowers like tiny white powder puffs. Summer. 60 cm (2 ft).*
S. sagittifolia	Similar in growth and habit to *S. japonica*, but with white blooms with black and rose centres. Late summer. 60–90 cm (2–3 ft).
Scirpus albescens	Handsome upright stems of glowing sulphurous white marked with thin green longitudinal stripes. 60 cm–1.20 m (2–4 ft).
S. zebrinus (Zebra rush)	A curious mutant with slender spiky rushes alternately barred with cream and green. 60–90 cm (2–3 ft.)
Typha angustifolia (Lesser reedmace)	Popularly known erroneously as the 'bulrush'. Slender glaucous foliage and handsome brown poker heads. Late summer. 90 cm–1.80 m (3–6 ft).
T. laxmanii	Slender willowy leaves and smaller brown poker heads. A most suitable and well proportioned 'bulrush' for the smaller pool. Late summer. 60 cm–1.20 m (2–4 ft).
T. minima	A tiny 'bulrush' with masses of short fat brown poker heads amidst a waving sea of grassy foliage. Late summer. 30–45 cm (1–1½ ft).

CHAPTER 6

FLOATING AND SUBMERGED AQUATICS

FLOATING AQUATICS

Floating aquatics have a different way of life to anything the gardener commonly encounters. Not only do they seldom produce roots for anchorage or absorption of plant foods, but most develop turions, or winter buds, and effectively disappear during the autumn. For this reason it is wise to keep a few in a bowl during the winter, so that they can be given a little warmth during early spring to encourage premature growth and shade the first flush of water discolouring algae, thus discouraging its growth. Allowed to remain in the cool waters of the pool, they take a considerable time to reappear and fulfil their role, and often fall prey to browsing water snails. Planting consists merely of tossing them on to the surface of the water.

Azolla caroliniana (Fairy moss)	A tiny floating fern with soft mossy foliage, lime green when young or growing in the shade, red in full sun and at the approach of autumn.
Eichhornia crassipes (Water hyacinth)	A tender aquatic of great beauty, usually grown as an annual and placed on the pool when all danger of frost has gone. Gorgeous lavender-blue orchid-like blooms in short spikes above curious glossy foliage with grossly inflated leaf bases. Summer.
Hydrocharis morsus-ranae (Frogbit)	Small white three-petalled flowers are borne amongst small floating kidney-shaped leaves. Summer.
Stratiotes aloides (Water soldier)	Dense rosettes of spiny dark green leaves like the top of a pineapple support clusters of creamy-white flowers. Summer.

Trapa natans (Water chestnut)	Rosettes of dark green rhomboidal floating leaves and unusual creamy-white axillary flowers. Technically an annual, it forms a 'nut' each autumn which falls to the bottom of the pool and does not reappear and germinate until the following spring. Summer.
Utricularia vulgaris (Bladderwort)	A fascinating rootless floating plant with trailing stems of fine whorled leaves that conceal tiny bladders which trap any unwary aquatic insects that dare to venture amongst the foliage. Striking spikes of yellow antirrhinum-like flowers held well above the water. Summer.

SUBMERGED OXYGENATING AQUATICS

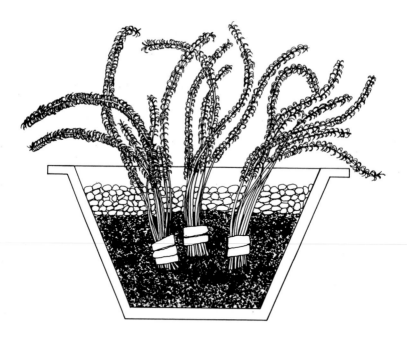

Fig. 13 Submerged oxygenating plants are usually sold as bunches of unrooted cuttings, fastened together at the base with a strip of lead, which acts as a weight to hold them down. The lead weight should be buried in the compost, otherwise it will rot through the stems and the plants will float to the surface. The compost is topped with a layer of pea gravel.

Astilbe 'Fanal' has some of the deepest coloured flowers of any of this charming family of bog garden plants.

Submerged oxygenating plants are those that we affectionately refer to as 'weeds', and their function is to maintain healthy, well-oxygenated water for the fish and other livestock. However, from the gardener's point of view they serve another purpose too, for all thrive on the same mineral salts as green water discolouring algae and, being more advanced forms of plant life, they are able to starve the algae out and ensure crystal clear water if planted in sufficient numbers at the outset.

Submerged oxygenating plants are usually sold as bunches of unrooted cuttings, fastened together at the base with a strip of lead. Although appearing to be clinging precariously to life, once introduced to the pool they quickly produce roots and become established. Apart from fastening the cuttings together, the lead strip acts as a weight to hold the bunch down. It is important when planting submerged oxygenating plants that this lead weight is buried in the compost (Fig. 13), or else it will rot through the stems and they will come floating to the surface. Some pool owners plant their submerged plants in containers full of pea gravel, but trays or proper planting containers of good clean heavy soil, topped off with a generous layer of pea gravel to prevent fish from stirring up the mud and fouling the water, are best.

Callitriche platycarpa (Starwort)	Dense tufts of pea-green underwater foliage, rising to the surface during the summer and affording shelter for fish and their fry.
Ceratophyllum demersum (Hornwort, coontail)	Dark green bristly foliage arranged in dense whorls around slender brittle stems. A good plant for shaded or deep water.
Elodea canadensis (Anacharis, Canadian pondweed)	A prolific plant with dense bushy stems bearing whorls of dark green foliage. An excellent oxygenating plant, but apt to get out of control in large or natural ponds.
Hottonia palustris (Water violet)	Bold whorls of striking lime-green foliage support erect spikes of lilac or whitish flowers. Early summer.
Lagarosiphon major	Long succulent stems densely clothed in broad dark green crispy foliage. Very much like an *Elodea*, and formerly well known as *Elodea crispa*.
Myriophyllum spicatum (Spiked milfoil)	Feathery trailing stems and spikes of very small crimson flowers just above water level.

M. verticillatum (Whorled milfoil)	Dense whorls of narrow submerged leaves and short spikes of insignificant greenish flowers.
Potomogeton crispus (Curled pondweed)	Handsome, serrated and undulating bronze-green transluscent foliage. Small crimson and cream blooms in short dense spikes.
Ranunculus aquatilis (Water crowfoot)	Flaccid, deeply dissected, submerged foliage closely resembling an out-stretched bird's foot. Floating clover-like foliage surmounted by tiny glistening gold and white chalices. Summer.

CHAPTER 7

THE BOG GARDEN

A bog garden is a natural extension of a pool in which moisture loving plants can be grown. Construction is not difficult when in conjunction with a pool, but its development should be envisaged when the pool and its immediate surroundings are planned. If the pool is to be made with a liner there is no difficulty, for all that need be done, is order the liner larger than needed for the pool and incorporate it at the edge as if it were a spreading shallow pool about 30 cm (1 ft) deep (Fig 14). A retaining wall of loose bricks or stones is then spread across the border between the pool proper and the bog garden, and the latter filled with a mixture of equal parts coarse peat and soil laid over a layer of gravel. This gives a moisture retentive medium, but allows excess water to

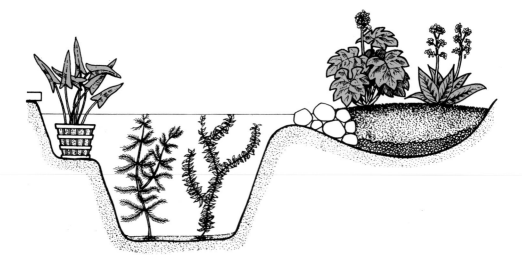

Fig. 14 Cross-sectional drawing of a pool incorporating a bog garden, showing how the butyl liner is used to contain the bog garden. The extra amount of liner needed to make the bog garden must be allowed for at the planning stage. The rocks or stones at the pool boundary retain the bog-garden soil yet allow water to percolate through from the pool.

drain from the roots. Water from the pool moistens the soil through the barrier, the soil surface being about 2.5 cm (1 in) above the mean water level. If the pool is to be of concrete a similar constrution in that material can be made. However, if a plastic or fibreglass pool is used a small independent polythene lined bog garden will have to be constructed.

Unlike true aquatic plants, those of the bog garden must be planted during the traditional planting season which extends from early autumn until late spring. Generally they are border plants of the usual herbaceous nature, which although needing plenty of moisture to grow prolifically, cannot tolerate standing water. Under ordinary border conditions they often become stunted and their leaves burned at the edges because they are too dry, so the only place in which they can be grown properly is a bog garden. Routine care consists of keeping weeds and pests under control, and the tidying up of superfluous foliage immediately the frost has cut it back in order to deprive aquatic insect pests of a winter refuge. Most bog garden and waterside plants should be divided during the dormant season every third or fourth year in order to maintain flower size and general vigour.

The measurements in the following section denote the average heights of mature plants.

BOG GARDEN AND WATERSIDE PLANTS

Aruncus sylvester 'Kneiffi' (Dwarf goat's beard)	Short white plumes above deeply cut pale green foliage. Summer. 60–90 cm (2–3 ft).
Astilbe arendsii	A charming group of hybrid astilbes with neat mounds of deeply cut foliage and feathered plumes of richly coloured flowers. Summer. 60–90 cm (2–3 ft). Popular varieties are 'Fanal' bright crimson, 'White Gloria' and the delicious salmon-pink 'Peach Blossom'.
Euphorbia palustris	A lush growing species of spurge with large greeny-yellow heads during late spring. 90 cm (3 ft).
Filipendula digitata	Coarse upright perennial with loose spikes of pinkish flowers. Summer. 60–90 cm (2–3 ft). Its diminutive variety 'Compacta' has mounds of bright green foliage and bright pink blooms. Summer. 30 cm (1 ft).

F. palmata	Stems of pale pink blooms above bright green leaves. Its variety *elegans* has similar white blossoms. Summer. 90 cm (3 ft).
F. ulmaria 'Aurea'	A golden leafed form of our native meadow sweet. Insignificant flowers which should be removed. 30 cm (1 ft).
Hosta albo-marginata	Wavy green leaves with cream edges. Whitish blooms. Summer. 75 cm (2½ ft).
H. minor alba	Sweetly scented dwarf form with white flowers. Summer. 30 cm (1 ft).
H. tardiflora	Small green leaves and lilac flowers. Late summer. 23 cm (9 in).
H. undulata medio-variegata	Soft green leaves heavily blotched and striped with cream. Whitish blooms. Late summer. 45 cm (1½ ft).
Houttynia cordata	Bluish-green heart-shaped leaves on reddish stems. Small conical white flowers. Summer. 45 cm (1½ ft). The cultivar 'Plena' has fully double blossoms.
Iris kaempferi (Japanese clematis flowered iris)	Tufts of broad grassy foliage surmounted by large clematis-like blossoms. Some of the best cultivars are 'Blue Heaven', rich purple-blue with yellow throat, 'Landscape at Dawn', double pale rose-lavender and 'Mandarin', deep violet. Summer. 60–75 cm (2–2½ ft).
I. sibirica	A useful group of iris with clumps of grassy foliage. The sky blue 'Perry's Blue' is universally known, as are the pure white 'Snow Queen' and purple 'Caesar'. Summer. 60–75 cm (2–2½ ft).
Lobelia cardinalis	Green foliage and spires of vivid red flowers. Summer. 75 cm (2½ ft).
L. fulgens	Beetroot coloured stems and crimson flowers. Summer. 75 cm (2½ ft).
L. vedrariensis	Green foliage flushed with violet. Violet flowers. Late summer. 60–90 cm (2–3 ft).

Lysichitum americanum (North American skunk cabbage)	Large cabbagy leaves preceded by golden Arum-like flowers. Spring. 30–60 cm (1–2 ft).
L. camtschatcense	A smaller flowering white species from Asia. Spring. 30–60 cm (1–2 ft).
Mimulus cardinalis	Attractive hoary foliage, and brilliant scarlet orange flowers. Summer. 45 cm (1½ ft).
M. cupreus	Coppery blooms and pale green foliage. Summer. 45 cm (1½ ft). Hybrid races such as 'Monarch' strain are multi-coloured and very popular, as is the tiny red 'Whitecroft Scarlet'.
Primula	Candelabra species and cultivars. Handsome plants with whorled tiers of flowers.
P. beesiana	Rich rosy-purple. Summer. 60 cm (2 ft).
P. bulleyana	Orange-yellow. Summer. 75 cm (2½ ft).
P. chungensis	Pale orange. Summer. 30 cm (1 ft).
P. helodoxa	Rich yellow. Summer. 90 cm (3 ft).
P. japonica	Bright crimson. Summer. 60 cm (2 ft).
P. pulverulenta	Rich crimson. Mealy flower stems. Late spring. 75 cm (2½ ft). 'Bartley Strain' is a selected strain with shell-pink blooms. Late spring. 60 cm (2 ft).
Primula	Other moisture-loving kinds:
P. denticulata (Drumstick primula)	Balls of lilac blooms on short stout stems. A white cultivar 'Alba' is sometimes grown Spring. 30–45 cm (1–1½ ft).
P. florindae	Like a giant cowslip. Soft yellow flowers. Summer. 90 cm (3 ft).
P. microdonta alpicola	Nodding bell-shaped yellow flowers. Mealy leaves and stems. A white form *alba* is even more beautiful. Summer. 45 cm (1½ ft).

P. rosea	Brilliant rose coloured blooms close to the ground. Spring. 15 cm (6 in).
P. secundiflora	Deep rose red. Late spring. 30 cm (1 ft).
P. vialii	Cylindrical spikes of red and lavender blooms. Summer. 30–45 cm (1–1½ ft).
P. waltoni	Ruby red flowers heavily powdered with white. Summer. 45 cm (1½ ft).
Rheum palmatum	Striking Chinese rhubarb-like plant with immense spikes of creamy-white flowers. The form *atrosanguineum* has crimson blooms. Late spring. 1.5–2.5 m (5–8 ft).
Rodgersia aesculifolia	Bronzy-green divided leaves, creamy-white panicles of flowers. Summer. 90 cm (3 ft).
R. pinnata	Olive green foliage, rose-pink panicles of flowers. Summer. 60 cm (2 ft).
R. tabularis	Pale green circular leaves and dense panicles of cream flowers. Summer. 90 cm (3 ft).
Trollius europaeus (Globe flower)	Attractive buttercup-like plants with distinctive globular blooms. 'Golden Queen' has golden yellow flowers while 'Orange Crest' is bright orange. Late spring and early summer. 75 cm (2½ ft).

Hosta sieboldii albo-marginata is valued for its striking architectural shape, its smart variegation and its profuse flowering.

CHAPTER 8

FISH AND OTHER LIVESTOCK

Fish and other livestock are essential in maintaining a healthy environment in the pool. Indeed, they are essential for the control of aquatic insect life (which otherwise disfigures aquatic plants) and the larvae of the mosquito, the adults of which plague the gardener on summer evenings. They are also much valued as an additional source of interest in the water garden, adding colour and life to the pool and providing entertainment for old and young alike.

Ornamental pool fish that are commonly sold to the pond owners usually live amicably together, irrespective of size or species. The only difficult character is the catfish, which during its formative life feeds upon aquatic insect life, but which will turn its attention to small fish and the tails of larger ones as it reaches maturity. Providing that the catfish is avoided, and no more than a total of 15 cm (6 in) length fish is introduced for every 0.09 square metre (square foot) of the surface area of the water, excluding the marginal areas, then few problems should be encountered. This is a maximum stocking rate. If the fish are required to breed, then a stocking rate of one/third of that, or 5 cm (2 in) of fish to every 0.09 square metre (square foot) of surface area, is

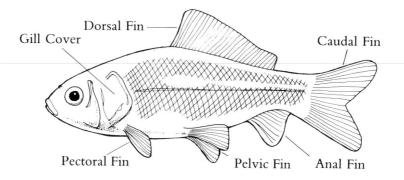

Fig. 15 Goldfish are the obvious choice when stocking a new pool. They provide a diversity of colour and shape not encountered in any other group of coldwater fish.

more satisfactory. The size of individual fish is not important. It is total combinaion of body length upon which the formula is based.

When stocking a pool with fish, take care to select healthy individuals with firm, meaty bodies and erect dorsal fins. It is important to wait until the plants have had time to become well established before introducing the fish, otherwise they will uproot the plants and dirty the water, and the entire pool will then go green as the uprooted plants are unable to function.

ORNAMENTAL POND FISH

There are many different kinds of fish that can be utilized in the water garden. The following selection are the most decorative and useful for the average garden pool.

Goldfish Everyone is familar with this popular orange, red or yellow fish which is frequently encountered in bowls and cold water aquaria indoors. The goldfish (Fig. 15) of the pool is exactly the same as the one we keep indoors as a pet and equally hardy. It is best to stock the pool initially with goldfish in a small size and allow them to grow, rather than be intent on creating an immediate effect with large individuals. Apart from the common goldfish there are those with long flowing tails called Comet Longtails.

Koi carp These are brightly coloured fish that are now becoming increasingly popular amongst pool owners. They are available in almost every colour imaginable and often have metallic or iridescent scales.

Orfe Both the silver and golden orfe make good pond fish, but it is the golden kind that is most frequently encountered. This is a slim bodied fish of an orange-gold colour, often with black markings on its head. Unlike the goldfish it is a surface swimmer, preferring to live in shoals. Golden and silver Orfes enjoy leaping for flies in the cool of the evening or else swimming vigorously against the flow of water from a waterfall.

Shubunkins These are really transparent scaled goldfish and have all the qualities of that species, but are available in a much wider colour range. Shubunkins are usually splashed and mottled in a multiplicity of colours, the blues of the Cambridge Blue and Bristol Blue Shubunkins being particularly fine.

Fig. 16 Scavenging snail: the ramshorn. This humble mollusc can be unreservedly recommended as it is hardy and lives exclusively on algae.

SCAVENGING FISH, SNAILS AND MUSSELS

Many pool owners believe that their pool will not function without scavengers. While it is true that scavenging fish and snails perform a valuable task, a well ordered pool can be equally well maintained without them. Scavengers, contrary to popular belief do not suck up mud and stones from the floor of the pool, but feed upon uneaten fish food and in the case of snails, on troublesome algae as well.

Tench This is the only scavenging fish that can be unreservedly recommended. The catfish that is sometimes suggested is carnivorous and pugnacious and generally creates havoc. The comon tench is of an olive-green colour, quiet and unassuming, spending most of its life unobserved on the floor of the pool.

Mussels Freshwater mussels perform a useful task in the established pool, sucking in algae-laden water, retaining the algae, and disgorging clear water. In a new pool they often die because the water has not matured and there is insufficient debris on the pool floor in which they can make their home. Two kinds are offered by water-gardening specialists, both of which are equally amenable. The painter's mussel has a yellowish shell with brown markings, while the swan mussel is brownish green with a white fleshy body.

Snails There are innumerable aquatic snails available for the pool, but it is only the ramshorn type (Fig. 16) that can be depended upon to restrict its appetite to undesirable algae. This is the snail with a flattened shell like a catherine wheel which the creature carries in an upright position on its back. All pointed snails should be regarded with suspicion as they have a liking for the foliage of aquatic plants. This especially applies to the large pointed snail known as the greater pond snail or freshwater whelk.

The bold yellow spathes of *Lysichitum americanum*, the skunk cabbage, a cousin of the familiar arum lily, are particularly striking.

CHAPTER 9

LOOKING AFTER THE POOL

Establishing a pool is initially time consuming, but once properly planted and stocked it is relatively undemanding compared with many other features of the garden. Routine care consists of keeping an eye open for pests and diseases along with the occasional division of aquatic plants. The propagation of plants and the breeding of fish are pleasurable pursuits that can also be followed.

THE POOL IN SPRING AND SUMMER

Waterlilies need lifting and dividing every few years. This is evident when there is a preponderance of leaf growth in the centre of the clump and flower size diminishes. Most popular waterlily cultivars need dividing every three or four years, although some of the smaller hybrids may go for six or seven years without requiring attention.

Late spring is the ideal time to divide waterlilies, the plants being lifted and the adult foliage removed at source. Most plants consist of a main rootstock from which several 'eyes' have grown to form sizeable 'branches', and it is these side growths that should be retained, cutting them from the parent with as much healthy young rootstock as possible. The thick bulky part of the original plant is generally of little use and should be discarded, but all the 'branches' can be planted individually to form new plants, providing that they each have a healthy terminal shoot.

Submerged oxygenating plants sometimes encroach beyond reasonable bounds and these too should be dealt with regularly. Many pool owners pull plants up by the handful and then wonder why the water turns green. Obviously, this is because the natural balance has been disturbed. A much more satisfactory method is to reduce the bushy foliage by about a third with a sharp knife or a pair of scissors. If the adult plants are looking weary, then these can be removed, the severed stems picked over, the healthiest pieces bunched together with a strip of lead or piece of wire, and then replanted in the vacant baskets. Marginal plants are divided in the same way as ordinary herbaceous perennials, using two hand forks back to back and prising the plants apart.

Feeding is an important factor in a successful pool. Waterlilies and marginal aquatics are all gross feeders and require regular treatment if they are to prosper. Unfortunately, difficulty is often experienced in getting fertilizer down to the roots without lifting and replanting in fresh compost or otherwise considerably fouling the water. Special sachets of aquatic plant fertilizer are currently available which can be merely pushed into the container beside the plants. These so-called 'pills' are made with a handful of coarse bonemeal and sufficient wet clay to bind it together. The frequency with which the operation is carried out depends upon the plants involved and the compost or soil in which they were originally planted, but its need becomes apparent when the leaves of the plant become yellowish and get progressively smaller, and the blooms are of poor colour and with few petals. Marginal plants can benefit considerably from this treatment, but it should not be provided for those of a rampant nature. Submerged oxygenating plants and floating subjects gain most of their nourishment directly from water, so attempting to feed them is time consuming and undesirable.

PREPARING THE POOL FOR WINTER

Algae seldom pose any problems during winter, for then the pool becomes dull and lifeless, but the preparation for this period of dormancy is with most pool owners a sadly neglected one. Untidy foliage at the water's edge provides a sanctuary for waterlily beetles and other aquatic pests, so should be removed as soon as the first autumn frosts turn it brown. Care should be taken when trimming rushes with hollow stems. as these will 'drown' if cut below water level, so sufficient length should remain to allow for a fluctuating water level.

Waterlilies can be allowed to die back naturally, but any leaves with soft, crumbling edges or spreading black blotches should be regarded with suspicion and removed, as they may well be infected by waterlily leaf spot. This is not a deadly disease, but does spoil established waterlilies. The new pool owner will almost certainly feel some concern for the waterlilies during the winter but, providing they are growing in a suitable depth of water, they will overwinter perfectly. Miniature waterlilies that may be growing in a shallow rock pool or sink should ideally have all the water drained off their crowns and then be protected by a generous layer of old leaves or straw. Once the danger of frost has passed, they can easily be restarted into growth by refilling the pool or sink. Remember to cover the empty pool or sink in the autumn, or it will rapidly refill from rain and snow.

All desirable free-floating aquatic plants disappear for the winter months, forming turions, or winter buds, which fall to the bottom of the pool until the warm spring sunshine stirs them into growth once again. If these are collected before they sink and are placed in a jar of water in a cool airy place, they will start into growth much sooner, and, by providing much needed surface shade, can do much to combat the algal growth that is invariably experienced in early spring.

Fish should be prepared for their winter vigil by judicious feeding with ants' eggs, dried flies or freeze-dried worms until the weather turns cold and they cease to be active. No further nourishment need be provided until they are seen swimming about once again in the spring. All popular kinds of decorative pond fish can survive for several months during the winter without feeding, as their body processes slow down in much the same manner as a tree or shrub in the garden becomes dormant. Likewise, they can stand extreme cold and will not suffer even if trapped beneath a layer of ice for a day or two.

Ice is the greatest worry that a pool owner has during winter months, for not only does it trap noxious gases which are likely to suffocate the fish, but it also exerts tremendous pressure upon the pool structure and can crack the most expertly laid concrete. The best way to prevent such damage occuring is to float a piece of wood or a child's rubber ball on the water, so that the ice exerts pressure against an object capable of expanding and contracting. If a submersible pump is used during the summer, then this can be detached and an electric pool heater installed in its place. This consists of a heated brass rod with a polystyrene float, and is perfectly safe to use, keeping an area of water clear of ice in the severest weather. Alternatively, during a spell of prolonged cold weather when one fears for the safety of the fish, a hole can be made in the ice by placing a pan of boiling water on the surface and allowing this to melt through. Never make a hole in the ice by hitting it with a blunt instrument as this will kill or concuss the fish.

PROPAGATING A FEW PLANTS

Waterlilies are quite easily propagated from 'eyes'. These are latent growing points which appear on the rootstocks of mature plants, sometimes appearing as young shoots and buds, at other times as rounded nodules. The form that they take depends upon the species of waterlily from which the variety has been derived. Eyes are removed with a sharp knife when the waterlily is lifted for division, ideally during late spring. Some eyes are easily detached, others have to be removed with a sharp knife. The wounds of both eyes and rootstocks

Primula bulleyana, one of the species of candelabra primula with several whorls of flowers on each stem, revels in wet soil.

should be dusted with charcoal or sulphur to help prevent infection. The adult plant can then be returned to the pool.

Severed eyes are best potted individually in good clean garden soil and stood in a shallow bowl of water with their growing points submerged. As the tiny leaf stalks of the young waterlilies lengthen, the water level must be raised. Potting of growing plants should be continuous until they attain a size where they can be transferred to the outdoor pool without hazard. It is important that when they are planted in their permanent position, that they are accommodated in proper waterlily planting baskets.

Some of the miniature waterlilies have to be increased from seed as they do not produce eyes. This particularly applies to the tiny white *Nymphaea pygmaea* 'Alba'. Seed must be gathered from freshly ripened seed pods. Dried seed will be most unlikely to germinate. When harvested correctly, the seed will be enclosed in a jelly-like material and this should be sown intact. Good clean garden soil is the best sowing medium, especially if it is inclined to be heavy and has been well sieved to eliminate stones, twigs and similar undesirable debris. Seed pans should be filled with this and the gelatinous material containing the seed spread as evenly as possible over the surface. A light covering of soil must be given and the pans watered with a fine rose attachment. They can then be placed in a bowl or aquarium with the water just over the surface of the compost.

The first seedlings will appear within a couple of weeks. They have tiny translucent lance-shaped leaves and resemble liverworts. From this stage until the plants are large enough to take care of themselves, filamentous algae may make itself a nuisance, becoming entangled in the delicate young foliage. Any of the proprietary algicides correctly administered will help control the problem, although when quantities of algae are killed in this manner it is advisable to remove dead material as this will decompose and pollute the water as well as encouraging the rotting of seedlings. When floating leaves start coming to the surface of the water the plants are ready for pricking out. They should be carefully lifted in clumps, teased apart, and then pricked out into conventional plastic trays and submerged so that the compost is about 2.5 cm (1 in) beneath the surface of the water. Individual plants can eventually be potted singly in small pots.

Seed raising is not a widely used method of increasing the majority of other pool plants, although one or two are more readily increased in this manner. The method used is largely the same as described for waterlilies, the condition in which the seed has been stored being absolutely critical in most cases. The pickerel, *Pontederia cordata*, must be sown while green, whereas the water plantain, *Alisma plantago-aquatica*, will grow if the seed is twelve months old. The water hawthorn, *Aponogeton distachyus*, will grow if sown straight away or if kept until the following year, but loses its viability if allowed to dry out completely.

Most creeping aquatics are increased from cuttings taken during the spring when the shoots are about 5 cm (2 in) long. These include brooklime, *Veronica beccabunga*, and the water mint, *Mentha aquatica*. Bog bean, *Menyanthes trifoliata* and the bog arum, *Calla palustris* are increased by chopping their scrambling stems into sections, each with a dormant bud. If these are placed in a tray of mud they sprout very quickly. The true reeds and rushes, along with many other marginal subjects, are increased by division. Split them in the same manner as ordinary herbaceous perennials, but do not cut the foliage too far back. Some marginal plants have hollow stems and if these are cut so severely that water can enter, they rot away.

RAISING YOUR OWN FISH

Most pool owners are thrilled if they can persuade their fish to breed successfully. All the fish that the average person is likely to have are of the carp family and have similar requirements for their successful reproduction, although certain species, such as orfe and tench, seem loath to breed in captivity in Britain. However, all the fish known collectively as carp and, of course, the common goldfish and its forms reproduce freely.

The breeding season lasts from late spring until late summer, depending to some degree upon temperature. Most goldfish and related fish are sexually mature in their second year, although adulthood is related more directly to size than age. Any goldfish 8 cm (3 in) or more in length should be capable of breeding. Most pool owners who wish to breed a few fish start by purchasing one or two matched pairs and, while this can be recommended, it does not follow that the pair purchased will breed with one another if there are other sizeable fish in the pool. Generally, like will breed with like, but hybrids in the carp family are common, and those of similar shape and constitution do interbreed.

Identifying the male and female fish is relatively easy in the spring. Body shape, when viewed from above, is oval and elliptical for the female, and slim and pencil-like for the male, the male being further enhanced by the white, pimple-like nuptial tubercles which are sprinkled over the gill covers and top of the head.

A thriving colony of *Primula pulverulenta*, another candelabra species, in a pleasant range of hues, with *Iris pseudacorus* behind.

Spawning takes place with varying frequency throughout the breeding season. During spawning the male fish chases the female around the pool and amongst the submerged plants, brushing and pushing furiously against her flanks. She then releases the spawn, trailing it in and amongst the stems and foliage of submerged plant life. The male milt, or sperm-bearing fluid, is distributed over the eggs which are then, hopefully fertilized. Once this has happened, it is advisable to remove some of the plant material covered in spawn away from the preying adults (who will promptly eat most of it if there is only sparse plant cover in the pool). It can be placed in an aquarium with pond water until the young fry are large enough to survive the rough-and-tumble of the garden pool. It is important, though, to use pond water in the aquarium, for this will then be of the same temperature and composition, and therefore not injurious to the spawn.

After three or four days the fry will be seen developing. First of all, they are difficult to detect as they are minute and resemble tiny pins clinging to the leaves and stems of submerged plants. After a couple of weeks they are recognizable as fish, sometimes transparent, sometimes bronze, but all eventually attaining their correct adult proportions and colours.

There are few problems for the pool owner with a desire to breed a new fish, particularly if he starts with healthy stock of good proportions. Indeed, if goldfish and carp are placed in a pool, providing that the proportion of males and females is reasonably balanced, they will probably breed with some measure of success of their own accord without the pool owner needing to become involved.

CHAPTER 10

COMMON POOL PROBLEMS

As with most other living garden features the pool is not without its share of troubles. The commonest of these is undoubtedly discoloured water. Green water of a consistency like pea soup is familiar to most pool owners, for even in well established pools this condition may occur for a few days during early spring when the water is warmed by the sun, so algae appears before the submerged oxygenating plants have had a chance to start growing again.

It is the oxygenating plants that provide the key to the problems, for greenness in the water is caused by thousands of minute primitive free floating algae feeding on the mineral salts that are present. When faced with competition from the higher forms of aquatic plant life, they die out through starvation, thus leaving the pool clear.

To ensure clarity from the outset, it is essential that earlier advice applies. Plant one bunch of submerged oxygenating plant to every 0.185 sq metre (2 sq ft) of surface area and provide shade with floating plants and waterlily pads over approximately one third of the surface area. The latter effectively reduces the amount of sunlight falling directly into the water and generally makes conditions inhospitable for the growth of algae.

Algicides are sold by many aquatic plant nurseries and garden centres and while these are effective for a short period of time, they are not a substitute for a properly balanced pool. Some are successful in temporarily clearing the water of fine suspended algae, while others will kill blanketweed and silkweed. In the latter case it is important to remove the dead algae as this will deoxygenate the water during its decomposition and may asphyxiate the fish. The advance in algicides in recent years has been considerable. Apart from the traditional kinds based upon potassium permanganate or copper sulphate, there are now dual algicides/fish fungicides and slow release kinds, available as a dissolving block kept more or less permanently in the pool.

Another kind of cloudiness is caused by the fish stirring up mud and sediment on the floor of the pool. Covering the bottom of the pool and the tops of the planting baskets with a layer of well washed pea gravel usually prevents this recurring.

Unfortunately, a blue or milky cloudiness is not so easily corrected. This is generally caused by a decomposing body or bodies polluting the water and is usually accompanied by an unpleasant smell. In all but the mildest of cases the pool should be emptied, any accumulated sediment on the bottom removed, and then refilled with fresh water.

Sometimes in country districts a pool will take on a purplish tinge, a curious slimy jelly appears around the perimeter, and the fish and plants start to die. This is invariably the result of a chemical spray having entered the pool, either as spray drift, or on the feet or plumage of wild birds bathing in the margins. While little can be done to control spray drift, by planting the margins thickly with irises and rushes the splashing of birds in the shallows can be eliminated. Once a chemical has entered a pond and caused widespread damage, it is essential to take everything out and scrub the entire pool several times, emptying and refilling with clean water before restocking with fish and plants.

PESTS AND DISEASES OF AQUATIC PLANTS

Several pests and diseases manifest themselves upon aquatic plants. While few are fatal, all are difficult to control because of the presence of fish. Thus no chemical cure can be recommended.

Waterlily aphis Several species of aphis attack waterlilies, but it is the true waterlily aphis that is the most devastating. In warm weather they reproduce at a prodigious rate, smothering not only waterlilies, but other succulent aquatics and causing widespread disfiguration of flowers and foliage. The only remedy is to regularly spray the foliage with clear water to dislodge the pests so that the fish can devour them. As part of the life cycle of this pest is spent as eggs on the trunks and limbs of cherry and plum trees, a winter wash of these with tar oil ovicide will reduce the incidence of attacks the following year.

Waterlily beetles A troublesome pest in some localities, but fortunately not yet widespread, it is the larvae of this insignificant little brownish beetle that strips the surface layer from floating lily pads and flowers causing widespread decay. The larvae are small, black, with distinctive yellow bellies. They appear at any time from mid-summer onwards. Forcible spraying with clear water to dislodge them is the only means of control in a pool full of fish, but good autumn management deprives the adults of decaying pool-side vegetation in which to over-winter.

China mark moths The most common of these is the brown china mark moth, an insignificant little fellow that lays its eggs on the floating foliage of waterlilies and other aquatics. The tiny caterpillars which emerge burrow into the underside of the foliage and then make small oval cases out of these leaves. The devastation caused by an infestation of these caterpillars is readily apparent, chewed and distorted leaves crumbling towards the edges, surrounded by floating pieces of rapidly decaying foliage. The beautiful china mark moth is less common, but an equally destructive pest. Instead of burrowing into the foliage it makes its home in the stems of aquatic plants. As spraying is out of the question, the pool owner must resort to gathering all damaged floating foliage. Even small floating pieces should be collected as these may contain caterpillars in the process of constructing their shelters.

Caddis flies The larvae of caddis flies cause extensive damage to the flowers, leaves and roots of aquatic plants, not only by feeding on them, but by gathering pieces which they mix with sand, sticks and other debris to create tiny protective shelters. It is impossible to spray against caddis flies, but pools where there is a reasonable fish population are seldom infested. Fish regard caddis fly larvae as a delicacy.

False leaf-mining midge A tiny creature which cuts a tracery of lines all over the surface of floating foliage. Forcible spraying with clear water is the best control.

Waterlily leaf spot Both of the leaf spots common in waterlilies have a similar effect, the foliage becoming brown and dry at the edges, eventually crumbling and wasting away. Removal and burning of diseased leaves gives some measure of control.

Waterlily root rot This is a devastating disease which is most commonly encountered in mottled leafed varieties of waterlily. The leaves and stems become soft and blackened and the root evil-smelling and gelatinous. Affected plants should be removed immediately when noticed. Compost in which they have been growing should also be removed.

PESTS AND DISEASES OF POOL FISH

A number of pests and diseases attack pool fish, but most can be

Primula denticulata, the drumstick primula, forms tight heads of lavender, white or crimson flowers in early spring.

avoided if new stock is quarantined before introduction to the pool. Few diseases are incurable, but when a fish is badly diseased it is kindest to destroy it. The simplest way to destroy an ailing fish is to hold it in a damp cloth and dash it smartly against a hard surface such as a concrete path.

Anchor worm This little parasite attaches itself to fish with a vicious barbed head. It appears as a tiny whitish worm, often coated in green algae, and is impossible to pull off without causing damage to the fish. Control is by holding the fish in a damp cloth and touching the parasites with a child's paint brush dipped in ordinary household paraffin. This kills the tiny parasite, which can then be withdrawn with tweezers and the wound treated by immersion in a solution of malachite green to prevent secondary fungal infection. The pool can be safely treated with a modern sterilant.

Fish louse There are a number of these parasitic crustaceans which attack fish, attaching themselves to various parts of the body, but usually infesting the gills. They are strange little creatures with a shell-like carapace and clinging feeler-like attachments. Holding infested fish in a damp cloth and dabbing the parasites with paraffin administered with a child's paint brush dislodge the pests. Routine dipping afterwards in malachite green solution is advisable. The pool can be treated with a modern sterilant.

Fish leech While a number of different leeches will be seen in the garden pool it is only the fish leech that causes any serious problems. This fastens itself to fish and sucks until it is gorged with blood, thereafter falling away to rest amongst aquatic vegetation while its meal is digested. Control is very difficult, although in badly infested pools a piece of raw meat suspended in the water will attract considerable numbers. Obviously because of the leech's habit of resting for periods without causing any trouble, this process will have to be repeated regularly in order to attract all the hungry leeches.

Fungus The various fungal diseases which manifest themselves upon fish are almost exclusively secondary infections, developing on areas of the body which have been damaged in some way. Only very occasionally is fungus observed on fish without damaged tissue. This is usually after the winter when fish are naturally a little run down, but in most cases it is quickly cleared up with a standard fungus cure preparation. In the past, sea salt has been the only recognized medication for such infections, but in recent years great strides have been made in our understanding of the various fungal infections and cures based upon methylene blue and malachite green are readily available and work simply and quickly. Affected fish are dipped in such a solution for a short period and then can be safely returned to the pool.

White spot disease This parasitic disease is very common amongst freshly imported ornamental fish. It can be devastating if left unattended, but modern white spot cures can clear it up without too much trouble. The disease appears as white spots or 'measles' all over the fish. Eventually continual reinfection by mobile parasites will kill the host. Really heavy attacks are incurable and badly infested fish should be destroyed. Otherwise, slightly affected fish should be isolated and put into a solution of white spot cure based upon quinine salts. If it is possible to raise the temperature of the water a little, the life cycle of the parasite will be hastened and a cure more quickly effected. Recently a remedy was introduced that can be added to the pond water and this is proving to be successful.

There are many more pests and diseases than described here, but the foregoing are the most likely to be encountered. In a well ordered and maintained pool these will in any event be minimal. The most important thing to remember when treating fish diseases is that the instructions on the container of the chemical cure should be strictly adhered to. An extra teaspoonful for luck could well be disaster.

DEALING WITH HERONS

Herons often make themselves a nuisance, even in quite densely populated areas. They spot their prey from the air and, having successfully visited the pool, continue to do so until all the sizeable fish have been taken. Herons generally fish at dawn before the gardener has stirred and it may be some time before the pool-owner is aware that his fish are disappearing. As herons fish while standing in the pool, it is a simple matter to deter them. Erect a small fence around the pool consisting of short canes abut 15 cm (6 in) high, linked toether with a single strand of fishing line. This will not be visible to the heron, who will touch it with his legs. After several attempts at different points around the pool, he will move on. Herons seem to be incapable of stepping over the deterrent. Netting is sometimes sold to keep herons at bay, but this is difficult to maintain in good order, as plants become entangled in it and look unsightly.

INDEX